· The Euro in Law & Practice ·

The Euro in Law & Practice

Editor
Birgit Ris
LLB, LLM
Solicitor with
Dibb Lupton Alsop
Brussels

Palladian Law Publishing Ltd

Published by
Palladian Law Publishing Ltd
Beach Road
Bembridge
Isle of Wight PO35 5NQ

www.palladianlaw.com

ISBN 1 902558 16 2

Typeset by Heath Lodge Publishing Services
Printed in Great Britain by The Book Company Limited

· Contents ·

· Preface ·

"It is perceived that the full benefit of political integration can only be achieved if conditions are created that would enable cross-border integration of markets for goods, services, capital and labour. The use of a single currency is a crucial vehicle for such market integration. It is a symbol and catalyst for political and social integration in Europe." This is a quote from a speech delivered by Sirkka Hämäläinen, a member of the executive board of the European Central Bank at the Nordic Forex '99, Helsinki, 21 August 1999 which briefly encapsulates the thinking behind the creation of a single currency. It is not just a mechanical development in the history of the European Union, but rather an economic, political and social advancement. As a result, neither non-participating Member States nor third countries can ignore the Euro or its impact on the whole legal framework.

This book deals with the legal aspects of the implementation of the Euro in areas such as banking and finance, pensions, tax, contract continuity, redenomination of share capital and information technology contracts. It also considers the complexities of the rounding rules between the Euro and national currencies.

Each chapter is self-contained, giving the reader both background and analysis of the particular subject area. The authors of the individual chapters are recognised experts in their fields of practice. They have given long and hard consideration to and researched extensively into the possible pitfalls and opportunities brought about by the Euro. I would also like to thank them for their hard work and the time and effort that went into their contributions without which this book would not have happened. I would also like to thank David Church for his assistance and valuable comments on the text. Finally, I would like to thank my publishers for their continuous encouragement and their saintly patience.

Birgit Ris
Brussels
September 1999

Dibb Lupton Alsop

· List of Contributors ·

Victoria Bright and Usha Jagessar

Information Technology

Clare Denison

Banking and Finance

Jeremy Harrison

Pensions

Trevor James

Tax Issues

Julia Stout

Redenomination of Share Capital

Duncan Gillespie

Continuity of Contracts

Mike Pullen

Rounding Rules
Euroland and the USA

Birgit Ris

History and Background
The Legal Framework

· Table of Cases ·

· Table of Statutes ·

· Table of EU Legislation ·

· History and Background ·

Why do we need a single currency, why create a single market? To quote from Napoleon: "Europe needs a single currency - it will be good for trade."

> "There is nothing new about the desire to unite Europe. Figures from history as diverse as the Roman emperors, Genghis Khan, Napoleon and Hitler have in turn coveted the common objective of taking the Continent as their own."[1]

The creation of the European Union aimed to achieve a lasting peace in Europe which historically none of the other European alliances had been able to sustain. The Union would be for the benefit of the citizens rather than part of a strategy to build an empire and would be achieved through co-operation. Its roots can be traced back to the end of the Second World War, when most of Europe had been devastated structurally, politically and economically by the two world wars. The time was ripe for change, to turn off the path of continuous turmoil to one which would lead to the integration of the European States. European integration was seen as a means to a more economically prosperous and politically secure Europe.

In 1951, Belgium, the Netherlands, Germany, Luxembourg, France and Italy signed the Treaty of Paris establishing the European Coal and Steel Community. The Treaty differed from the previous types of international treaties in that it established new institutions which were independent from the Member States and were specifically mandated to fulfil the obligations under the Treaty. The institutions were created to supervise the development of the Member States' coal and steel industries. Even then the Treaty was based on more than just pure economics as can be seen from the Preamble which when referring to the creation of the Treaty describes it as "the basis for a broader and deeper Community among peoples long divided by bloody conflicts".

---

1 Weatherhill, Stephen & Beaumont, Paul, *EC Law*: the essential guide to the legal workings of the European Community, (2nd ed) Penguin Books.

In 1957 the Treaty of Paris was followed by the two Treaties of Rome:[2] the European Economic Treaty (EEC) and the European Atomic Energy Community (Euratom). Like the Treaty of Paris these Treaties led to the creation of independent institutions. In effect, however, although there were three separate Treaties and three separate Communities the day-to-day administration was run as one.

The EEC Treaty was much broader in scope than the Paris and Euratom Treaties. It advocated the creation of a single market by removing restrictions and barriers to trade and the abolition of obstacles to free movement of capital, persons and services between the Member States. Procedures were established to facilitate the passing of legislation. The institutions established to carry out the legislative procedure were the Commission, the Council of Ministers and the Assembly (which later became known as the European Parliament).

For nearly 30 years the EEC Treaty remained unchanged until the signing of the Single European Act in February 1986. Among other matters it confirmed the Member States' commitment to further integration and the development and completion of a single European market by the end of 1992. This was to be realised by "approximation of the Member States' laws", *i.e.* harmonisation, standardisation, regulation and eventual liberalisation. The "1992" programme culminated in the creation of the legal framework ensuring the removal of most physical and technical barriers to trade within the EU. Its success created further impetus for greater economic and monetary co-operation.

February 1992 saw the signing of the European Union Treaty, otherwise known as the Maastricht Treaty, under which the EEC was renamed the European Community (EC). The Treaty further enlarged the scope of the Community competence and strengthened the decision-making process by giving more power to the European Parliament. It provided for full economic and monetary union and committed the Member States (*i.e.* Belgium, Germany, Spain, France, Ireland, Italy, Luxembourg, the Netherlands, Austria, Portugal and Finland) to the creation of a single currency by 1 January 1999.

---

2 Only Belgium, the Netherlands, Germany, France, Italy and Luxembourg were original signatories. Further signatories to the EEC Treaty joined in 1973: the UK, Denmark and the Republic of Ireland; Greece in 1979; Spain and Portugal in 1986; Finland, Sweden and Austria in 1995.

Economic and Monetary Union

Running parallel with the evolution of the Treaties was the consciousness of eventually creating a Monetary Union. Although it was not specifically mentioned until the EU Treaty was signed in Maastricht it had, in fact, been a loosely recognised goal since the signing of the EEC Treaty in 1957. A Monetary Committee had in fact been established in 1958 to consider the possibility of establishing a co-ordinated monetary policy.

As the Community progressed by establishing a customs union and a common commercial policy the idea of a single currency grew in popularity. It was, however, several events, such as the collapse in the 1960s of the Bretton Woods system of fixed exchange rates and the Europe-wide recession which convinced the original six Member States to press for economic and monetary union (EMU). A European Council Summit was held in 1969 declaring closer union between the Member States including monetary union and a further committee was established to consider the EMU. Their findings resulted in the Werner report[3] which was submitted to the Council and Commission in 1970.

The Werner report

Attempts were made as early as the 1970s to establish a basis for monetary union. The Werner report proposed a three-stage approach to achieving this. First, the creation of a currency snake, which was implemented in 1972 and was supposed to limit the exchange rate flexibility in which the value of participating currencies could fluctuate by ± 1.125% of a centrally-fixed parity. Secondly, the establishment of a European central bank; and thirdly, harmonisation of economic policies. The currency snake, however, became unsustainable and was abandoned in the late 1970s, following the oil crisis and recession in Europe. Furthermore, Germany and France differed over the method to be used in arriving at EMU. The French had difficulties in linking the Franc to the Deutschmark and accepting the corollary of Bundesbank influence over French monetary policy. In 1979, at the instigation of Germany, negotiations were resurrected. The new proposal for an exchange rate mechanism was much less ambitious. The Germans accepted some French influence over

---

3 Named after the Prime Minister of Luxembourg.

monetary policy, and the French eventually accepted the de facto linkage with the German Deutschmark. Thus the European Monetary System (EMS) was established.

European Monetary System

The EMS was launched in 1979. It was by no means a monetary union but it was essential in preparing the ground for fostering greater stability between Member States` currencies, stronger co-ordination and convergence of their economic and monetary policies. It was basically made up of three identifiable components:

(1) The European currency unit (ECU). The ECU was the notional euro currency which was based on a trade-weighted basket of all the EU currencies. The ECU only served as an accounting and reference value for transferring credits within the EMS, for accounting units for the EU`s budget and for currency transactions between companies based in the Member States and as a form of security for the issuing of ECU bonds on international currency markets.

(2) The Exchange Rate Mechanism (ERM). The ERM was at the heart of the EMS in that it provided for "fixed but adjustable" exchange rates between the currencies. The ERM resembled the currency snake of the 1970s in that it was a system where the exchange rates of a currency fluctuated within a prescribed margin. This was a centrally fixed rate of exchange which was set when a Member State joined the EMS. The ERM helped to stabilise participants` exchange rates and the frequency of changes of parity steadily declined between 1979 and 1995. On occasions Member States, like the United Kingdom and Italy due to domestic pressures, were forced to step out of the ERM.

The currency of participating Member States, in the ERM, has a band defined around each of its bi-lateral central rates and another band defined around its ECU central rate. This was decided as a compromise between France who wanted the exchange rate band to be defined around ECU and Germany who wanted the exchange rate band to be defined bi-laterally.[4] In 1996 the Commission issued a communication to the Council proposing measures to ensure the

4 Emmanuel Appel, *European Monetary Integration 1958-2002*, Routledge (London & New York).

effective operation of the ERM. The model proposed a so-called "hub and spokes" model, with the Euro being the hub and the national currencies the spokes. Therefore, the Member States joining the first wave would be within the first spoke and more closely aligned to the Euro than those Member States not within the first wave of the Euro.

(3) The European Monetary Co-operation Fund (EMCF). This organisation provided credit facilities to Member States` central banks.

The EMS was not a monetary union. It merely helped prepare the ground for discussions and negotiations between the Member States in formulating the creation of EMU. By comparison EMU:

- was built on the notion of a single currency;
- was created by Treaty;
- replaced the currencies of all participating Member States; and
- established a European Central Bank responsible for a single monetary policy and encouraging closer convergence of economic and fiscal policies.

Furthermore, the Member States participating in the EMS retained their currencies and control of national monetary policies which is not the case with the EMU.

European Monetary Union

By the time the Maastricht Treaty was being negotiated in 1990-91, the EMS was widely regarded as a success by both economists and politicians. Besides the drop in volatility of exchange rates between the European currencies, there was also increasing convergence of both inflation rates and long term interest rates. The success of the EMS was significant, in that it provided the background to the discussions on Economic and Monetary Union (EMU) which were resurrected in the late 1980s. This, coupled with other factors, led the Member States to recognise that in order to complete the EU`s goal of a single market, EMU would need to be implemented.

Following the signing of the European Single Act in 1986, the Member States agreed in 1988 to set up a committee to study European Monetary Union. This committee was set up and conducted under the chairmanship of Jacques Delors (the then President of the European

Commission). The following year the committee submitted the Delors Report to the Council. When the Council met in Madrid, in 1989, they endorsed the report and declared that the first stage of EMU would begin in July 1990. It proposed a three-stage plan which would introduce and eventually provide for greater co-ordination of economic and monetary policies, the establishment of a single currency and the setting up of a European Central Bank.

By endorsing the Delors Report the Member States committed themselves to guaranteeing the gradual abolition of all restrictions on the free movement of capital and a move towards economic convergence. The principle of free movement of capital was already enshrined in the Treaty of Rome but the political will in the Member States needed to be mobilised. Economic convergence was a new objective for the EU which required more detailed provisions. These were finally incorporated in the Treaty on European Union signed in Maastricht in 1992.

At its meeting in Maastricht in December 1991, the Council defined the conditions and the timetable for the introduction of the EMU. This was to be achieved in three stages: Stage I had already begun in July 1990, as noted above, following the Council's agreement to the Commission's report at Madrid in 1989. Stage II, the Council would begin in January 1994 and Stage III no later than 1 January 1999.

Stage I

Stage I required the removal of remaining restrictions on the free movement of capital within the EU. This was further extended to include the unrestricted free movement of capital between the EU and third countries. Member States were encouraged to focus on economic convergence and, where necessary, adopted multi-annual convergence programmes. The programmes were continuously monitored and assessed by the Council of Economic and Finance Ministers (ECOFIN). These programmes were designed to ensure the attainment of sustained low inflation, sound public finances and exchange rate stability among the Member States. These measures were the preparatory steps towards the adoption of the Euro.

Stage II

Stage II started in January 1994 and terminated in December 1998 had the following objectives:

- Based on a recommendation from ECOFIN to decide which of the Member States would meet the convergence criteria to qualify for participation in EMU. This decision was in fact taken in May 1998.[5]
- To decide whether it would be appropriate to move on to Stage III and if so to set a date for its commencement. This was confirmed at the Madrid Summit held in 1995, where the Council decided it would be appropriate to move towards Stage III and set the date for 1 January 1999.
- To set out a detailed framework for the establishment of a European Monetary Institute (EMI). EMI was the forerunner of the European Central Bank.
- To encourage Member States to avoid excessive government deficits. This was not a legally binding commitment and the provisions could not be enforced during Stage II. The Commission monitored the Member States for compliance with the following criteria:
  (i) actual and planned government deficits must not exceed 3%;
  (ii) total government debt must not exceed 60% of the Member States' GDP.
- Member States were requested to enact the necessary measures to ensure the full independence of the national central banks.
- The adoption of legislation prohibiting monetary financing of public sector activities. This meant that both the public sector entities and the Member States could no longer turn to the central banks for credit; similarly, a prohibition was also imposed on the direct purchase of a public debt by the central banks. Later these measures would also be extended to include the ECB.
- The adoption of legislation prohibiting the public sector entities from gaining privileged access to financial institutions.
- The adoption of legislation which would prohibit the assumption of the public sector liabilities of one Member State by another.

As has already been stated, the European Council decided, at the Madrid Summit in 1995, that it was appropriate to move towards

---

5 It recommended that Belgium, Germany, Spain, France, Ireland, Italy, Luxembourg, the Netherlands, Austria, Portugal and Finland would form the Euro area from 1 January 1999.

Stage III which could begin on 1 January 1999. The EMI, which was already in operation, had an important role to play in the move towards Stage III of EMU.

Mr Lamfalussy, a Frenchman, was elected and appointed by the Member States as head of EMI. The other members of EMI included representatives of the Member States' national central banks. EMI, which was governed by a Statute contained in the Protocol attached to the EU Treaty (Maastricht), was required to:

- carry out the groundwork for EMU by preparing the necessary instruments for a single monetary policy;
- determine the framework for the setting up of the European system of central banks;
- produce reports on Member States' compliance with the convergence criteria for the purposes of determining who in its view would be eligible to join Stage III;
- report on the Member States' progress in amending the relevant legislation, securing the independence of their national central banks in accordance with the EMI Statute and the Treaty;
- monitor the EMS, to co-ordinate monetary policy and encourage the co-ordination between national central banks.

Stage III

It was the task of the Council (ECOFIN), on the basis of reports prepared by EMI and the Commission, to decide by a qualified majority which of the Member States would meet the convergence criteria prior to the beginning of Stage III. From the beginning of this stage the Euro became legal tender and the conversion rates between the participating Member States' currencies and the Euro were irrevocably fixed. Euro bank notes and coins, however, would not be issued until 1 January 2002. In the meantime the national currencies of Member States remain in circulation and retain their legal status. Stage III established the creation of three new monetary institutions:

- the European Central Bank (ECB) which would eventually take over the functions of the EMI;
- the European System of Central Banks (ESCB); and
- the Economic and Financial Committee which took over the tasks and responsibilities from the Monetary Committee which was originally set up in 1958.

These three institutions have a powerful role in the Community monetary policy decision-making.

The European Central Bank

The European Central Bank is one of the key players in shaping and deciding on Community monetary policy. It is be responsible for:

- defining and implementing the monetary policy of the Community;
- conducting foreign exchange operations pursuant to Article 109 (new Article 111);
- holding and managing the official foreign reserves of the Member States;
- promoting the smooth operation of payment systems;
- the issuing of bank notes with legal tender status within the Community;
- collecting the necessary statistical information in order to undertake these tasks of the ESCB.[6]

The ECB is headed by a governing council which comprises of the governors of the central banks of the Member States participating in Stage III and the members of the executive board of the ECB. The executive board consists of the President, the Vice-President, and four other appointed members. The ECB was launched on 1 December 1998 and is headed by a Dutchman, Wim Duisenberg. He, and the other members of the executive board, will serve an eight-year term. All members of the governing council will be completely independent and neither the Council, Commission nor the Parliament will have any decision-making role in the ECB. The President of the Council and a member of the Commission may participate in meetings of the governing council, but they have no right to vote. The ECB has to report to the Commission once a year and Parliament may request the ECB to appear before it if so requested. The ECB also has the capacity to fine undertakings which fail to comply with the ECB regulations or decisions.

6 The framework for the operation of the European System of Central Banks, presentation for the Society of Advanced Legal Studies Conference on "Economic and Monetary Union - a comparative perspective on public and private law issues", Martin Thomas, Senior Legal Counsel, Financial Law Division, European Central Bank, 22 January 1999.

In addition to, and not to be confused with, the governing council, it should be noted that the ECB also has a general council, which co-ordinates the monetary policy of those Member States which are as yet outside the single currency area, until such time as they do join.

European System of Central Banks

The ESCB is composed of the ECB and the national central banks (NCB) of all 15 Member States of the EU, and became operational at the start of Stage III on 1 January 1999. Unlike the ECB, the ESCB does not have a legal personality even though each of the individual NCBs does. The ESCB is also independent and is governed by the decision-making bodies of the ECB which consist of the ECB's governing council and the executive board. The primary role of the ESCB is to maintain price stability and it is also responsible for defining and implementing Community monetary policy. The ESCB is also charged with the responsibility of holding and managing the official foreign reserves of the Member States, promoting the smooth operation of EU payment systems, and conducting foreign exchange operations. Furthermore, it will also be responsible for supervising credit institutions and the stability of the financial system.

Primary Community legislation

The prime source of legislation governing the ESCB and the ECB is contained in the Protocols to the Maastricht Treaty. The Maastricht Treaty provides procedures for the establishment of an ESCB, its powers are therefore restricted to the provisions set out in the Treaty and the Statute (Treaty, Article 4A – new Article 8).[7]

The Maastricht Treaty provides for two categories of Member State in respect of the EMU. The first category consists of the Member States who have fulfilled the necessary criteria for the adoption of the Euro by 1 January 1999 (as mentioned above and participate in EMU). The second category consists of those Member States which do not qualify for membership and those which have opted-out of participation. Member States who do not participate have fewer rights and

---

7 *Op cit*, fn 6.

obligations arising from the Treaty and the Statute pertaining to the adoption of the Euro, such as being permitted to vote on Council decisions regarding Stage III matters. The United Kingdom and Denmark have notified the Council that they do not as yet intend to participate in Stage III. The special status of the United Kingdom and Denmark is recognised in Protocols to the Maastricht Treaty, which note that the United Kingdom will not be obliged or committed to move to Stage III without a definite decision to do so by its government and Parliament, and that the Danish constitution may require a referendum to be held before Denmark could participate in Stage III.

The ECB fulfils its tasks and responsibilities in part by adopting certain "legal acts" to facilitate the smooth running of the monetary policy in the Community. Legislation will be in the form of Regulations, and Decisions. It will also issue Guidelines, Recommendations and Opinions. The Regulations will have a general application and direct applicability binding on the participating Member States. The Decisions will only be binding on those to whom they are addressed. Guidelines and instructions will constitute a formal legal instrument but with a limited scope; the Recommendations and Opinions are non-binding legal acts.

The Economic and Financial Committee

The Economic and Financial Committee replaces the existing Monetary Committee (originally established in 1958) and will be responsible for monitoring the economic situation in the EU and for submitting regular reports to the Council. The Member States, the Commission and the ESCB will each appoint no more than two members of the Committee.

The convergence criteria

The convergence criteria as set out in the Maastricht Treaty established which Member States would be allowed to participate in Stage III according to the following measures:

- sustainable inflation - must not exceed by more than 1.5% the three averaged lowest rates in the EU taken from the previous year;
- budget deficits must be less than 3% of the GDP;
- overall public debt must not exceed 60% of the GDP;

- no currency devaluation should have take place within the Exchange Rate Mechanism for the preceding two-year period;
- the long-term average interest rates over the previous year must not exceed the three averaged lowest rates in the EU by more than 2%.

Before coming to its conclusion the Council also took into consideration reports prepared by the Commission and EMI on the development of the ECU, the results of the integration of markets, balance of payments and the development of various price indices, such as unit labour costs.

The stability and growth pact

ECOFIN held an informal meeting in Dublin in September 1996 where broad agreement was reached over the terms of the stability and growth pact (the Pact). The final terms of the Pact were agreed by the governments in Amsterdam in June 1997 and it is designed to ensure that convergence continues after 1 January 1996.

The Pact refers to the fiscal measures required to ensure that members of EMU continue to adhere to fiscally prudent policies. The Ministers agreed that the Pact should require a medium budgetary balance which will be the goal for Stage III participants and that measures must be agreed implementing budgetary discipline. The Commission proposed that the participating Member States would pledge to keep their budget deficit below 3% of GDP. Furthermore, it was suggested that Members be given a 10-month time frame in which to correct any budget deficits from rising above the 3%. If there was no improvement after the initial 10 months, Members would be required to place interest-bearing deposits with the Commission. If the deficit continued to be greater than 3% for two years in total the Council may agree by a two-thirds majority to fine the Member concerned up to 0.05% of GDP.

> "The application of these principles would involve a two-track strategy:
>
> 1. a preventative early warning system for identifying and correcting budgetary slippages before they bring the deficit above the 3% ceiling; and

2. a dissuasive set of rules with sufficient deterrent effect to put pressure on Member States to avoid excessive deficits except under exceptional and temporary situations or to take measures to correct them quickly if they occur."[8]

Single currency

Designs agreed for the Euro currency have created seven notes. Euro notes will be in denominations of 5 (grey), 10 (red), 20 (blue), 50 (orange), 100 (green), 200 (yellow and brown) and 500 (purple) Euros. The notes will include a security thread and a watermark as well as a special ink which enables the note to change colour depending on the angle at which it is viewed and raised print. Common to the notes will be the name of the currency, the Euro, the EU's 12-star emblem and the signature of the President of the ECB. Preparation of the Euro notes is the responsibility of the EMI, while the Member States' governments and mints have the responsibility for coin design and production. The Euro coins will have one common side and one "national" side. The Euro currency is to be delivered to EMU participants' central banks from the middle of 2001 to be in circulation by 1 January 2002.

Banknotes and coins

The Regulation provides that the bank notes and coins of the national currency unit retain their legal status during the transitional period (*i.e.* until 31 December 2001). There is then an extension for a further six-month period. However, any Member State is permitted to shorten the six-month breathing space and it is believed that many will do so.

The changeover from the national currency unit to the Euro bank notes and coins shall take place on 1 January 2002 as decided in accordance with the Madrid Meeting.

Article 12 obliges the participating Member States to ensure that adequate action has been taken to exterminate counterfeiting and falsification of bank notes and coins. Most Members have ratified the Geneva Convention on the Protection of Bank Notes which provides for protection not only of national bank notes but also those denominated in other currencies.

---

8 *Op cit*, fn 4.

Legal status of the Euro

The legal framework of the Euro is dealt with more fully in Chapter 1. This chapter deals with the two Regulations now in force – Council Regulation (EC) No 1103/97 and Council Regulation (EC) 9255/97. However, the most significant measures provided for by the Regulations are as follows:

- as from 1 January 1999 reference to the ECU in any legal instrument shall be replaced by the Euro at a rate of 1:1;
- contracts which are denominated in ECU or national currencies of participating States extending beyond 1 January 1999 will remain legal and enforceable;
- rounding rules are introduced and exchange rate rules on conversion to the Euro are defined;
- a "no compulsion/no prohibition" doctrine is introduced, meaning all are free to use the Euro if they can but there is no obligation to do so. After the Euro is introduced in 2002, however, parties will have to use the Euro.

The effect of the introduction of the Euro on continuity of contract is explained in greater detail in Chapter 7. National laws will remain in force and contract obligations remain enforceable during the transition period of 1 January 1999 to 31 December 2002. In relation to contracts, the choice of using the Euro, national currencies or the ECU also remains during this transitional period.

Birgit Ris

*Chapter 1 **

· The Legal Framework ·

1.1 Introduction

1 January 1999 was a landmark date in the history of the European Union. It is the date on which the 11 participating Member States adopted the Euro as their national currency. This core provision of the monetary law of the European Union was provided for in the third stage of the Economic and Monetary Union (EMU) as set out in the Maastricht Treaty[1] (the EU Treaty). The main provisions for the legal framework for the introduction and the use of the Euro are set out in two Council Regulations, namely:

- Council Regulation (EC) 974/98 of 3 May 1998 on the introduction of the Euro.[2] This Regulation was based on Article 109 I(4) of the EU Treaty (new Article 120) which deals with the monetary law provisions not dealt with by Regulation 1103/97; and
- Council Regulation (EC) 1103/97 of 17 June 1997 on certain provisions relating to the introduction of the Euro[3] which is based on Article 235 of the EU Treaty (new Article 308). It entered into force on 20 June 1997, and is the first Regulation dealing with the single currency, the Euro. The Regulation is binding and directly applicable in the whole European Community.

1.2 Preparatory work

In May 1995 the Commission published a Green Paper on the practical arrangements for the introduction of the single currency in which the

1 Maastricht/EU Treaty signed in December 1991.
2 The Ecofin Council decided on 7 July 1997 to publish the draft Regulation in OJ 1997 C236.
3 OJ 1997 L162.

* This chapter was written by Birgit Ris, Dibb Lupton Alsop, Brussels

principal issues relating to the legal framework of the Euro were identified. The Green Paper established the basis for both Regulations. It addressed issues such as the definition of the status of the single currency and of the national currency unit, the definition of legal tender, the continuity of contracts, the rounding rules and provisions for bank notes. In Madrid in December 1995, the European Council of Ministers decided on the legal framework for the introduction of the Euro and agreed that:

> "The Council Regulation entering into force on 1 January 1999 will provide the legal framework for the use of the Euro. From that date the Euro will be 'a currency in its own right' and the official ECU basket will cease to exist. This Regulation will have the effect that the national currencies and the Euro will become different expressions of what is economically the same currency. As long as different national monetary units (NCUs) still exist, the Council Regulation will establish a legally enforceable equivalence between the Euro and the national currencyeunits ('legally enforceable Equivalence' means that each monetary amount is assigned, in a legally enforceable way, an unexchangeable countervalue in terms of the Euro unit at the official conversion rate and vice versa). For the period before the deadline set for the completion of the changeover, the Regulation will ensure that private economic agents will be free to use the Euro; at the same time they should not be obliged to do so. As far as possible they should be allowed to develop their own mechanism of adjustment to the changeover; however, the implementation of these principles should take into account market practices in terms of standardisation. The Regulation will also provide that national bank notes will continue to remain legal tender within the boundaries of the respective national territories until the completion of the changeover to the single currency. The technical preparatory work for this Regulation shall be completed at the latest by the end of 1996."[4]

Subsequent to the Council's decision the Commission put forward its proposals in October 1996. The proposals were based on the Commission's extensive consultation with industry and substantial input was made by the European Monetary Institute (EMI).[5] The Commission undertook extensive consultations with the banking industry, consumers, employers' organisations, retailers and vending associations. The banking sector was concerned in particular with the

---

4 OJ 1996 C22.
5 The precursor of the ECB.

provisions relating to continuity of contracts, the conversion of the ECU basket and on rounding rules. What above anything else these consultations made clear was that there was an urgent need for legal certainty that not only required timely preparation but also timely implementation of the legal framework.

It quickly became apparent that Article 109 I(4) (new Article 120) was not able to fulfil the industry's demands. It would only be possible to use Article 109 I(4) of the Treaty for the adoption of "the other measures necessary for the rapid introduction of the Euro" when all the participating Member States could be known. As this would not be certain for some time it was agreed at the Council of Ministers for Economic Affairs and Finance (Ecofin) meeting in Dublin in September 1996 to separate the legal framework into the "provisions requiring the urgent legal certainty" which would be based on Article 235 (new Article 308) and "the other monetary law provisions" on Article 109 I(4) (new Article 120).

When the meetings in Dublin concluded two issues remained outstanding:

(1) The precise date for the introduction of the Euro bank notes and coins; and

(2) The redenomination of outstanding debt.

It was agreed that the precise date would be decided "in accordance with the Madrid scenario, when this Regulation is adopted", which would not be before Spring 1998. With regard to redenomination Ecofin finally reached a compromise in June 1997 which was the result of discussions with financial markets' representatives and the Member States.

The Regulation based on Article 109 I(4) (new Article 120) was not adopted until 1998 when the participating Member States were known. Prior to this, however, the draft could be relied upon to the extent that the European Council had given its blessings in Dublin and Amsterdam and that the text could be relied on to organise the preparatory works necessary.

1.3 Regulation 974/98 on introduction of the Euro

Legal status of participating Member States' national legislation of currencies during transitional period

The Regulation, based on Article 109 I(4) (new Article 120) contains the main part of the monetary law of the participating Member States. It defines the status of the Euro as a single currency and the legal status of the national currencies during the transitional period. The Regulation provided in Article 2 that the Euro would become the legal currency of the participating Member States as from 1 January 1999. From that date the national currencies did not entirely disappear but will continue to exist as a denomination of the Euro until 2002 when they will cease to exist. As the Euro notes and coins will not be available until January 2002 national currency units continue to be used during the transitional period between 1 January 1999 to 31 December 2001. The Regulation sets out how, during the transitional period, the Euro will exist in several denominations:

(1) The Euro unit itself and its sub-division, the cent.
(2) The national currency units which will exist as a sub-denomination of the Euro.

This, therefore, means that during the transitional period there will be the Euro as the currency of the participating Member States and the national currency units as denominations of the Euro. During the three-year transitional period the Euro will not only be divided into the cent (1 Euro = 100 cents) but also into the national currency units according to the conversion rates.

Actual Euro bank notes and coins will not be circulated until January 2002 (the end of the transitional period). In the meantime the Euro will only exist in the form of book money and cash payments will have to continue to be made in the national currency.

"No compulsion/no prohibition"

The principle of no compulsion/no prohibition is an important part of the formation of legal instruments during the transitional phase. In order to accommodate this freedom of choice the Regulation has provided for a number of rules protecting the "no compulsion/no prohibition" principle. It ensures that economic agents are free to use whatever currency they choose and that there is no obligation to use the Euro unit. The no-compulsion/no prohibition principle is enshrined in Article 8 of the Regulation. Articles 2 and 6 of the Regulation confirm that both the Euro unit as well as the national currency unit can be used to set up valid legal instruments, such as contracts. The unit which the parties have decided on must continue to be respected by both the parties unless they both agree otherwise. For example, if a contract is set up in DM (Germany being one of the Member States participating in Stage III beginning on 1 January 1999) all statements of accounts, invoices etc will continue to be made in DM unless the parties agree otherwise.

Article 8(2) ensures the "no compulsion/no prohibition" principle by providing that only those parties who have specifically agreed to use the Euro would be obliged to do so. Thus, legal instruments created before 1 January 1999 have not automatically changed their denominations during the transitional period. Therefore in the example above, a contract originally drawn up in DM will remain a contract written in DM but of course DM has become a denomination of the Euro.

Article 8(5), like Article 8(2), also provides for protective measures in accordance with the no compulsion/no prohibition principle stating that the use of the Euro unit may only be imposed in accordance with Community legislation. The provision extends beyond contractual relationships and includes all transactions whether public or private such as tax declarations and publishing accounts. Therefore, those who wish to complete such documentation in the Euro unit are free to do so.

There are, however, three exceptions to the principle of "no compulsion/no prohibition". These are provided for in Article 8(3) and (4) of the Regulation. The first exception deals with special provisions regarding payments by crediting an account, the second relates to re-denomination of debt and the third exception to Member States taking measures to allow organised markets to change their units of account.

(1) The Regulation creates special provisions for payments when crediting an account. Payments made within the participating Member State can be made by the debtor either in the Euro unit or that of the national currency unit. Recital 13 of the Regulation, however, provides that this "should not imply that financial intermediaries are obliged to make available either other payment facilities or products denominated in any particular unit of the Euro". If the payment has not already been converted by the

sending bank, then the receiving credit institution is obliged to convert the incoming payment into the denomination of the account of the creditor. This does not require the authorisation of the account holder. The provision applies to all types of payments including payments by cheque and other debit instruments.

(2) The second special provision concerns the re-denomination of debt. Re-denomination simply means changing the unit in which the debt is expressed from the national currency unit into the Euro unit. Article 8(4) gives Member States the right to re-denominate their outstanding general government debt, without having to seek the creditor's consent. This would only apply to a general government debt which is denominated in their national currency unit and issued under their own law. Once the government of a Member State has effectively re-denominated its public debt, or at least part of it, other issuers, whether private or public of securitised debts, have under Article 8(4) a unilateral right to re-denominate their outstanding debt. Take, for example, a Belgian issuer of an Italian debt under French law. The Belgian can re-denominate his debt once the Italian Government has either fully or partially re-denominated its own debt. In order for the Belgian to carry out the re-denomination of Italian debt it would not require consent from the investors.

(3) The Regulation provides for Member States to take the relevant action necessary in facilitating organised markets, such as stock exchanges and systems for regular exchange, clearing and settlement of payments to change to the Euro unit.

Article 8(5) states that the basis for any further possible exceptions can only be provided for by Community legislation. However, during the transitional period the national legislator is permitted to maintain the necessary provisions which require the use of the national currency unit. National legislation, however, may not interfere with the principle of "freedom of contract" and it can therefore not forbid the use of the Euro unit.

Bank notes and coins

The Regulation provides that the bank notes and coins of the national currency unit retain their legal status during the transitional period (*i.e.* until 31 December 2001). There is then an extension for a further six-month period. However, any Member State is permitted to shorten the six-month breathing space and it is believed that many will do so.

The changeover from the national currency unit to Euro bank notes and coins shall take place on 1 January 2002 as decided at the Madrid Meeting.

Article 12 obliges the participating Member States to ensure that adequate action has been taken to eradicate counterfeiting and falsification of bank notes and coins. Most Members have ratified the Geneva Convention on the Protection of Bank Notes which provides for protection not only of national bank notes but also those denominated in other currencies.

Final changeover

At the end of the transitional period the national currencies cease to exist. After this the Euro unit and the cent as its sub-unit will be the only legal tender, replacing the national units of the participating Member States. In accordance with Article 14 all references to the national currency unit in legal instruments existing at the end of the transitional period will be replaced by the Euro unit. A physical re-denomination in the legal instrument is not immediately necessary. It is, however, recommended to do so with regard to long-term contracts.

As mentioned above Member States have up to six months after the end of the transitional period, *i.e.* until 30 June 2002 at the latest, after which their national currency loses its legal tender status. During this six-month period Member States are free to implement the necessary rules and regulations to facilitate the withdrawal of their national currency and to introduce fully the Euro unit. The Regulation, however, does not discuss the issue of fees which may arise as a result of converting from national currency to the Euro.

1.4 Council Regulation 1103/97 on certain provisions relating to introduction of the Euro

This Regulation, based on Article 235 (new Article 308), deals with those matters for which the financial markets demanded legal clarity.

ECU-Euro conversion

Article 2 of the Regulation confirms conversion between the official ECU, on the bases of 1 ECU = 1 Euro. This provision establishes what has already been stated in the Treaty and by the European Council in Madrid in December 1995. The conversion not only applies to the ECU as referred to in Article 109G (new Article 118) but also applies to contracts under private law that make specific reference to the ECU.

Furthermore, the Regulation states that all references to the ECU are to be taken as defined in European Community legislation. The reason for inserting this provision was to clarify the assumption that most parties, when referring to the Euro, mean the ECU as defined in Community legislation even if this was not accurately reflected in the wording of their legal instruments. This provision is of course notwithstanding any contractual provisions to the contrary. The rebuttal need not be in writing but can also be deduced from the parties' conduct in the negotiations or from other relevant factors. The presumption, however, that all references to the ECU are as defined in Community legislation modifies the burden of proof for the parties in that the burden lies with the party claiming that the reference to the ECU was something other than that defined in Community legislation.

Continuity of contracts

Confirmation of continuity of contract is enshrined in Article 3. This principle had already been established by the European Council in the Madrid meeting and was supposed to provide greater transparency. The Article refers to "Introduction of the Euro" which encompasses a much broader concept than the mere substitution of the Euro for the national currencies. As far back as the Green Paper in 1995, the Commission has advocated that the introduction of the Euro would not lead to the frustration in respect of legal instruments. This applies to principles of similar effect such as *Wegfall der Geschäftsgrundlage*, *Théorie de l'imprévision*, etc. In order for these principles to apply, in most jurisdictions, the following conditions would need to be satisfied:

(1) There must be a severe disruption of the circumstances underlying the contract, which goes beyond the general acceptable risks to be carried by one of the parties.

(2) The event must have been unforeseeable.

It can therefore be concluded that this would not be the case in most existing legal instruments. Furthermore the Regulation provides a clear declaration confirming the continuity of contracts.

Although the European Community cannot legislate for third countries, the confirmation of the principle of contract continuity provides some reassurance for these countries. However, even if this was not the case the application of the principle of *lex monetae* would ensure the continuity of existing legal instruments denominated in national Member State currencies which have been substituted by the Euro. Further to the principle of *lex monetae* the State of New York legislature has in fact enacted legislation stipulating that the introduction of the Euro including any references to interest rates, would not lead to a discharge or excuse performance under any legal instrument nor would it lead to the right of any party to alter or terminate unilaterally any legal instrument.[6]

Reference rates

Rounding/conversion rules

The Regulation also provides for rules on rounding and on the use of the conversion rates. The rules, which are the product of work carried out by the EMI and the national central banks, are meant to ensure a high degree of accuracy when making conversions. The conversions should be such that it does not result in profit. The official conversion rates which were not adopted until 1 January 1999 have in fact been fixed for some time. One Euro is used to convert to the participating Member States currency, *i.e.* one Euro[7] equals 39,2345 BEF. The conversion rates are always represented by six figures and when making the conversion should never be rounded-off or truncated. The official conversion rates are to be used both between the Euro and the national currency units and also for conversions between the national currency units of participating States (which latter has to be undertaken using triangulation – see below and Chap 3).

When converting a national currency to the Euro it has to be divided by the conversion rate and when converting from the Euro to the national currency one has to multiply by the respective conversion rate.

---

6 See Chap 9.

7 The currency "UER" was allocated to the single currency by the ISO 4217 maintenance agency responsible for currency codes on 21 April 1997.

Inverse rates are never to be used because the associated rounding of the rate would give rise to inaccuracies in multiple conversions. This would be of particular relevance when converting large sums. Although the Council has fixed rates between the national currencies and the Euro, no such rate is fixed for converting between the national currencies. Instead the Council has provided a fixed algorithm which provides an explanation as to how conversion between one national currency to another should be calculated. First, the national currency is to be converted to the Euro. Secondly, the Euro is converted into the other national currency. Again the reason for calculating the conversions in this manner is to avoid profit-making and to maintain the highest degree of accuracy possible. Article 4(4) does not exclude the use of alternative methods of calculation provided the results are identical to that used when using the algorithm.

Chapter 3 deals with the rounding/conversion rules in more detail.

*Chapter 2**

· Banking and Finance ·

2.1 Introduction

This chapter looks at the practical consequences of European Economic and Monetary Union (EMU) and the Euro for companies based in the United Kingdom who:

- import and/or export goods and services from/to countries in the Euro zone (*i.e.* Belgium, Germany, France, Spain, Ireland, Italy, Luxembourg, the Netherlands, Austria, Portugal and Finland); and/or
- take out foreign currency loans.

Whilst jargon is kept to a minimum in this chapter, a glossary of terms often used in connection with European Economic and Monetary Union is set out in the Appendix to this chapter.

2.2 Background to EMU

European Economic and Monetary Union

By signing the Maastricht Treaty in February 1992 each member of the European Union committed themselves to European Economic and Monetary Union. Central to this commitment was the adoption of a single European currency – the Euro – which, subject to Member States complying with various economic and other criteria (the so called convergence criteria) would be implemented across Member States on a specified date.

The United Kingdom and Denmark famously negotiated various amendments – or in press parlance "**opt outs**" – to the Maastricht Treaty securing for themselves (amongst other things) the right voluntarily not to participate in the Euro until they elect to do so.

On 1 January 1999 each national currency unit of countries participating in the Euro (*e.g.* French francs, pesetas etc) ceased to be

* This chapter was written by Clare Denison, Partner, Dibb Lupton Alsop.

the economically independent currency of the corresponding participant country and became instead a non decimal denomination of the Euro and for all practical purposes the Euro became the new single currency of the participating States on that date.

Each old currency unit, however, continues to exist in the physical sense (*i.e.* as notes and coins) as legal tender in the relevant participating country and will continue to do so for a specified period – since initially at least, no Euro coins or notes are in circulation and none will be until early 2002. Old currency units have not, however, become legal tender outside the corresponding participant Member State. Deutschmarks, for example, are not legal tender for the settlement of Euró obligations in Belgium. In law, the old currency units are part of the Euro and their value in Euro is fixed at the official conversion rate announced on 31 December 1998 as follows:

1 Euro	=	1.95583	Deutschmarks
		6.55957	French francs
		2.20371	Dutch guilders
		166.386	Spanish pesetas
		200.482	Portuguese escudos
		1936.27	Italian lire
		40.3399	Belgian francs
		.787564	Irish pounds
		13.7603	Austrian schilling
		5.94573	Finnish markka
		40.3399	Luxembourg francs

With effect from 1 January 1999, all 11 participating States share a common monetary policy for which the newly established European Central Bank based in Frankfurt is responsible. The European Central Bank is also responsible for setting Euro interest rates. The Euro is legal tender but until Euro notes and coins are in circulation, its use is necessarily restricted to cashless transactions.

What does it all mean in practice?

These are the main principles of the Euro but what does it mean in practice? The fact that the old national currency units are still physically present and in circulation and the fact that (amongst others), banks and newspapers continue to quote exchange rates for sterling against the old currency units means that the advent of the

Euro has, in the United Kingdom at least, passed without too much seeming to change. For many in the United Kingdom, the Euro is undoubtedly as invisible in everyday life as its predecessor, the ECU or European Currency Unit. Some examples may help to illustrate the change:

- an existing contract for goods and services and which stipulates payment in French francs, for example, is now a contract for goods and services stipulating payment in Euros denominated in French francs;
- a request to a bank foreign exchange cashier for "£200 worth of Deutschmarks" is now in fact a request for "£200 worth of Euros (at the then current exchange rate of sterling against the Euro and which that bank is quoting) denominated in Deutschmarks";
- a price ticket in a shop in France quoting a price of "FF500" is in fact a price equal to the Euro equivalent of FF 500 to (at the official conversion rate) and payable in French francs;
- a request to a bank foreign exchange cashier to exchange an amount of French francs into Spanish pesetas is in fact a request to the cashier to change the denomination of the Euro equivalent of the French francs at the official Euro/French franc conversion rate from French francs to Spanish pesetas. This process consists of two steps: first, a conversion of the French francs into Euros at the official Euro/French franc conversion rate; and secondly, a conversion of the amount of Euro into Spanish pesetas at the official Euro/peseta conversion rate.

The UK perspective

The United Kingdom opted not to adopt the Euro on 1 January 1999 (although it may join later). As a result sterling continues (in broad terms) to be an economically independent currency. The Bank of England continues to be solely responsible for setting sterling interest rates and, together with the Government, for the monetary policy of the United Kingdom. The value of sterling against the Euro on the international money markets will fluctuate, just as sterling used to fluctuate against the old national currencies of the Euro zone.

Three important dates

There are three important dates to remember:

(1) **1 January 1999** being the date on which:

- Germany, France, Italy, Luxembourg, the Netherlands, Spain, Portugal, Ireland, Austria, Belgium and Finland adopted the Euro as their single currency;
- the official conversion rates between the national currencies of the countries noted above were irrevocably fixed;
- the Euro became a currency in its own right and the national currency units of the countries listed above became non-decimal denominations of it; and
- the European Currency Unit or ECU was converted into the Euro at a conversion rate of 1 Euro for 1 ECU.

(2) **1 January 2002** or "E Day" being the latest date on which Euro notes and coins will be introduced into circulation and at which point the Euro will cease to be restricted to cashless transactions and will exist in a physical form (notes and coins) alongside the old national currencies which will continue in circulation as legal tender until 30 June 2002 (at the latest). During this period the old currency units will be gradually removed from circulation and replaced with Euro notes and coins. E day also marks the day on which contracts denominated in a national currency unit will be converted by operation of law into Euros and signals the beginning of the final stage during which old currency units will gradually be removed from circulation and be replaced by Euro notes and coins.

(3) **1 July 2002** which marks the end of the transition phase and is the latest date on which the old national currency units will cease to be legal tender of the relevant Member State.

No extra time

It is important to realise that E Day and the end of the final stage, *i.e.* the current timetable could apply to any country entering into European Economic and Monetary Union (such as the United Kingdom) after the first wave unless a special agreement is reached – thus reducing the length of the transition period and the length of time British business, for example, will have to prepare for the Euro. Although the British Government has indicated that the United

Kingdom will not join for the duration of this current Parliament (which in theory could last until 2001), a week is a long time in politics and this position could change. It seems unlikely, however, that if the United Kingdom were to join, the Government would agree a timetable which would not give all affected sectors sufficient time in which to prepare.

2.3 Importing and exporting

Effecting payments

No compulsion, no prohibition principle

If you are a business involved in the export of goods and/or services to a country in the Euro zone and/or the import of goods and/or services from a country in the Euro zone, then the currency in which payment under each relevant contract, trade or transaction may be legally effected and discharged at any time after January 1999 and prior to the commencement of the final stage will depend on the following:

- the currency in which payments are required to be made as stipulated in the relevant contract, trade or transaction;
- whether payment is required to be made or may be made in cash, *i.e.* physical delivery of actual notes and coins or by another cashless method, *e.g.* cheque, telegraphic transfer (TT) or other form of automated cashless credit transfer;
- whether or not the relevant contract, trade or transaction was in existence on 1 January 1999;
- any express provisions stipulated in the relevant contract, trade or transaction dealing with the Euro;
- the governing law of the contract, trade or transaction.

Taking each of these in turn:

The currency in which payments are required to be effected as stipulated in the relevant contract, trade or transaction

Contracts requiring payment in a currency which is not the national currency unit of a country which has adopted the Euro are not affected by the introduction of the Euro notwithstanding that the parties to them may be resident in a country which has adopted the Euro. Only contracts, trades or transactions where a national currency unit of a country participating in the Euro is the contractual currency are affected by the introduction of the Euro. This is true whether or not the parties to the relevant contract, trade or transaction are resident in, or trading from a participating country.

Contracts where payment is required to be made or may be made in cash

At all times prior to the introduction of Euro notes and coins it goes without saying that payment in cash can only be effected in a national currency unit. Accordingly, and by way of example, payment under a contract, trade or transaction specifying the contractual currency as Deutschmarks and for payment in cash only can only be discharged in Deutschmarks. In the case of a contract, trade or transaction where the Euro is expressed to be the contractual currency the correct national currency unit in which payment in cash may be made will be the national currency unit in the place of payment. The place of payment for these purposes will in turn depend on the terms of the contract and the governing law of the contract. After the introduction of Euro notes and coins and at all times prior to the end of the final stage but subject to any express provision in the relevant contract, trade or transaction to the contrary (see below) payments may be effected legally in Euros or in the relevant national currency unit.

Contracts where payment is required to be made or may be made otherwise than in cash

The position in relation to a contract, trade or transaction under which payments are not made in cash is not so simple and certain rules apply – the basic rule being that, during the transition phase (presently scheduled to end on 31 December 2001) the use of the Euro in contracts as the stipulated currency in which payments are denominated and/or required to be made to be effected is neither prohibited nor compulsory. Which rule applies depends on whether the relevant contract, trade or transaction was in existence on 1 January 1999.

Contracts in existence on 1 January 1999

In relation to contracts which were in existence on 1 January 1999 and which are denominated in the national currency unit of a participating State, the regulations provide that the payment obligations thereunder shall, unless the parties agree otherwise, be discharged by payment in that national currency unit provided that where the amount payable is to be effected by the debtor crediting an account of the creditor located in the corresponding Member State then the debtor can, instead, elect to pay in Euros. If a debtor elects to do so, the regulations stipulate that the creditor's bank is obliged to credit the amount to the account of the creditor in the currency of denomination of his account, such conversion being effected at the official conversion rate. The parties to a contract may not contract out of this provision. Contrary to first impressions, this provision does not contradict the basic "no compulsion/no prohibition" rule because the creditor will still receive the payment in the denomination originally agreed. The provision, therefore, essentially underlines the basic principle that national currency units shall be treated as being equivalent to and indistinguishable from the Euro and vice versa.

It is important to realise that this unilateral right of a debtor is only available when payments in a national currency unit of a participating Member State are to be made to an account of the creditor within that Member State, *i.e.* and not outside it so that the provision will not permit for example a peseta debt to be paid in Euro or vice versa if payment is to be made to a peseta denominated account located in Germany. In addition, since it will only apply where payment is made to an account and only where the debtor knows where the creditor's account is located, it does not extend to payments made by cheque.

Contracts coming into existence after 1 January 1999 but prior to 1 January 2002

In relation to contracts coming into existence during the transition period, freedom of contract applies and it is up to the parties to decide whether the contract should be denominated in a national currency unit or the Euro and what the currency of payment will be. To the extent that the contract, trade or transaction is silent on a particular point, the rules and regulations set out above will apply.

Governing law of the contract

It is important to note that all EC Regulations in relation to the Euro such as the no compulsion/no prohibition principle are binding in all Member States whether or not that Member State is also a participant in the third stage of EMU and therefore, are directly applicable in the United Kingdom. They do not extend, however, outside the Member States and therefore, may not be recognised in other jurisdictions.

The final stage

At all times after 31 December 2001 the Euro will have only one denomination – the Euro unit. Any obligation denominated in a national currency unit of a participating Member State will on 1 January 2002 be converted automatically into an obligation to make payment in Euros.

Decisions for the UK-based import and export business

Companies who are involved in cross-border trade with counterparties located in participating Member States will, therefore, need to decide and agree the terms which will apply to contracts entered into during the transition period. In relation to contracts already in existence and which are denominated in the national currency unit of a participating Member State, the company will be able to take advantage of the no prohibition/no compulsion principles outlined above so that unless it agrees to do so, it cannot be required to make payments in Euros and may continue to make them in the relevant national currency unit. However, this cannot prevent a customer or a supplier seeking to renegotiate the terms of an existing contract to provide for payment in Euro. The relative bargaining powers of the respective parties will be the deciding factor in who gets their way. Indeed, you may have no choice if your business is one to which an applicable convention applies – in that scenario you will be obliged to adjust and follow convention.

In the event that you agree either to invoice others or to be invoiced in Euro, consideration will need to be given to whether or not to open a Euro denominated bank account to facilitate the receipt and payment of Euros. Agreeing to be invoiced in Euros will not automatically require the opening of a Euro bank account. If the Euro business effectively replaces business hitherto contracted in a national currency unit then switching to the Euro may enable you to consolidate bank accounts denominated in those other national currency units.

At all times prior to E day it will not be possible to withdraw or gain access to Euros in the physical sense from the Euro account since no Euro note or coin will be in circulation to facilitate this. Any value can only be accessed in cash by converting an amount standing to the credit of the relevant account into a national currency unit at the conversion rate or into sterling at the then sterling/Euro exchange rate.

Exchange rate risk

The exchange rate risk for a UK-based company entering into a contract for goods and/or services for payment denominated in the Euro or in a national currency unit of the Euro is the same, namely an exposure to movements in the Euro/sterling exchange rate which will need to be managed and hedged either internally as part of a company's internal treasury management and cash and currency pooling or externally by making use of the treasury products on offer from any one of the clearing banks.

2.4 Conversion and rounding

Calculations

The official conversion rates between the Euro and the national currencies of the participating Member States were set irrevocably on 31 December 1998 and became applicable on 1 January 1999. The rates are set out above at page 12. Conversion and rounding rules apply which must be used when effecting conversions between the Euro and any national currency unit. Although the United Kingdom is outside the Euro zone, the rules are binding in the United Kingdom in respect of conversions between the Euro and national currency units carried out in the United Kingdom. However, the rules do not necessarily apply outside the European Union and they do not apply to the conversion of Euro into sterling and vice versa.

The regulations are designed to ensure legal equivalence, *i.e.* that so far as possible, the Euro and the national currency units in which it is denominated are indistinguishable.

Conversion

The rules in relation to conversion are as follows:

(1) The conversion rates shall not be rounded or truncated when making conversions.

(2) The conversion rates shall be used for conversions either way between the Euro unit and the national currency units. Inverse rates derived from the conversion rates shall not be used.

(3) Monetary amounts to be converted from one national currency unit into another shall first be converted into a monetary amount expressed in the Euro unit, which amount may be rounded to not less than three decimals and shall then be converted into the other national currency unit. No alternative method of calculation may be used unless it produces the same results.

It is not an offence as such not to follow the prescribed regulations but complying with the regulations is the only way of ensuring that any given converted amount is the legal equivalent of another denomination of a single currency.

For example, a party to a contract may decide to exercise its option to pay an amount due thereunder in French francs in Euros. If that party does not adhere to the regulations when calculating the amount of Euros required in order to discharge the debt denominated in French francs, it is at risk of either overpaying or underpaying the amount due.

Taking each of the conversion regulations in turn:

No rounding or truncating

It follows that, for consistency, the conversion rates must not be truncated or rounded in calculations. To do so would produce an "approximate" calculation rather than an accurate one.

No inverse rates

The regulations prescribe that the Euro conversion rates be adopted as one Euro expressed in terms of each national currency unit, *e.g.* 1 Euro = "x" Deutschmarks rather than the other way round or "inversely", *e.g.* DM = "x" Euro. Using an inverse rate leads to inaccuracies which arise as a result of the rounding of the inverse rate itself.

Triangulation

The regulations recognise that there will still be a requirement to convert one national currency unit into another. The prescribed method by which this is to be done is called "triangulation". As the name suggests, there are three stages to each conversion. To illustrate the regulation – a conversion of an amount of Deutschmarks into French francs:

- **Stage 1**. The Deutschmark amount is converted into Euros by dividing the amount of Deutschmarks by the Euro/Deutschmark official conversion rate (and not by utilising the inverse conversion rate) and rounding the product if necessary (rounding is not compulsory) to three decimal places.

- **Stage 2**. The Euro amount is then converted into French francs at the Euro/French franc conversion rate.
- **Stage 3**. The product of Stage 2 is then rounded in accordance with the rounding rules (see below) to the nearest centime.

Rounding

The Regulations provide as follows:

> "**Article 5**
>
> Monetary amounts to be paid or accounted for when a rounding takes place after a conversion into the Euro unit pursuant to Article 4 shall be rounded up or down to the nearest cent. Monetary amounts to be paid or accounted for which are converted into a national currency unit shall be rounded up or down to the nearest sub-unit or in the absence of a sub-unit to the nearest unit, or according to national law or practice to a multiple or fraction of the sub-unit or unit of the national currency unit. If the application of the conversion rate gives a result which is exactly half-way, the sum shall be rounded up."

The rounding regulations are similarly binding in Member States including the United Kingdom when converting amounts denominated in Euro into national currency units and vice versa but are borne not so much out of a desire to achieve accuracy as sheer practicalities. Where a person is obliged to pay an amount of Euro denominated and converted into a national currency and vice versa, it will be clearly necessary to round to the nearest unit of the national currency or Euro, as the case may be, since it is impossible to pay a fraction of a centime or a Euro unit.

The regulations provide that the rounding Regulation is to be applied wherever amounts are "to be paid or accounted for".

On the surface the Regulation seems clear enough but rounding can produce rounding differences and discrepancies which will need to be formally reconciled. For example, conversion and reconversion of amounts can give rise to rounding differences. This may arise where a debtor exercises his right to make payment of an amount stipulated to be paid in Euro in a national currency unit instead and vice versa under the no compulsion/no prohibition principle discussed above and the receipt is converted back into Euro or the relevant national currency, as the case may be. Similarly, rounding differences may arise when instalment payments are made and converted on a case-by-case basis --

the cumulative total of the individual sums not producing the same result as the total amount payable converted at the relevant rate.

Provision for an agreement as to the basis on which necessary reconciliations should be effected will therefore need to be addressed by parties to contracts to deal with this issue.

2.5 Impact on international financial contracts

The impact of EMU and the introduction of the Euro on cross-border financial contracts under which payments are to be made in a national currency unit of a country which has adopted the Euro is, in essence, no different to the impact of the Euro on any other contract denominated in a currency unit of a country which has adopted the Euro and which are discussed earlier in this chapter. The currency of that contract changed from the relevant national currency unit to the Euro on 1 January 1999 with all the consequential impact that has in terms of payments under it going forward. However, there are a number of specific issues which are of particular concern and/or peculiar to financial contracts. In addition, in relation to certain contracts, such as those relating to certain derivative products, the impact has been to remove the commercial rationale for the contract and/or render the contract totally meaningless such as a currency swap where both currencies involved are EMU participating currencies.

The main concern surrounding financial contracts has been in relation to the legal issues relating to continuity of contract, *i.e.* the fear that the introduction of the Euro would give a party to a contract (contrary to the other party's wishes) the ability at law unilaterally to terminate or vary the contract in question and pure commercial issues connected to whether performance would now be economically different and/or more burdensome for the party in question where no right to terminate the contract as a result exists. Taking each issue in turn:

Main issues

Continuity of contract

Continuity of contract under English law is dealt with at length elsewhere in this book (see Chap 7) and is not repeated here since the principles which apply to contracts in general which are governed by English law apply equally to financial contracts governed by English law. However, in relation to financial contracts in particular, the Financial Law Panel established a working group of commercial lawyers to look in detail at particular sections of the financial markets and the kinds of contract those markets utilise to assess whether consequences of the Euro specific to certain provisions in those contracts or to those contracts in general, such as: a dramatic change in interest rates impacting on fixed rate obligations undertaken pre-EMU, the disappearance of price sources (*i.e.* reference rates) and the disappearance of the commercial rationale for a financial contract could give rise to a situation where the continuity of contracts governed by English law could be called into question.

The working group published its findings in January 1998 in a paper entitled "Economic and Monetary Union: Continuity of Contracts in English Law". Essentially, the Financial Law Panel could identify no classes of transaction or form of contract governed by English law commonly used in financial and commercial markets where the principle of continuity of contracts is likely to be called into question by EMU.

In relation to Member States of the European Union, a Regulation applies which makes it clear that the occurrence of EMU will not, of itself, cause contracts to be frustrated or otherwise to become terminable early but is expressed to be subject to a contrary agreement between the parties, thus preserving freedom of contract. There is also a concern that a typical *force majeure* clause in a contract may, depending on the circumstances, operate to negate the effect of this Regulation. A typical *force majeure* clause is a provision which will allow one party unilaterally to terminate the contract in question because of the occurrence of an event outside the control of the party seeking to terminate, which event renders performance (by the party seeking to terminate) under the contract impossible.

It should be noted, however, that, continuity of a contract is governed by the governing law of the particular contract and although whilst it is unlikely that EMU and the Euro will affect English law contracts, this may not be the position under other laws.

You may have been asked to enter into an amendment to a contract containing such a provision in the run-up to the introduction of the Euro, such amendment providing expressly that the occurrence of an event associated with European Economic and Monetary Union in the European Union shall not constitute *force majeure* for the purposes of the relevant contract. Similarly, parties to contracts relating to sterling obligations may find such "precautionary" provisions in the contract designed to cover the possibility that sterling may join the Euro at some point in the future.

Interest rates and price sources

Interest rates

Fixed. Regulations applicable in EU Member States provide that the introduction of the Euro will not affect fixed interest rates. This means that a fixed rate agreed in relation to a loan in a national currency unit and which was pertinent to that national currency will continue notwithstanding that it may not (post EMU) reflect the Euro interest rates. This could be disadvantageous to a borrower if the fixed rate is above the Euro rates currently applicable. Since the Euro rate (at the time of writing) is comparatively low there is a significant chance that a number of loans taken out pre-EMU will fall into this category. Of course, agreeing to a fixed rate for a fixed duration is always a bit of a gamble. A borrower company in this position will need to decide how best to resolve the situation, bearing in mind that a prepayment or refinancing if permitted is likely to trigger break costs.

Floating. The issue with floating interest rates stems from the fact that the introduction of the Euro has resulted in certain commonly used price sources disappearing along with their reference currency. Companies that have borrowed affected currencies from the London market are likely (but not necessarily) to have done so at a floating rate determined by reference to LIBOR (the London Interbank Offered Rate) (whether it is in turn determined by reference to certain named "reference banks" or to a screen rate such as Reuters or Telerate). A company which has borrowed an affected currency locally (such as French francs on the Paris market) is likely (though not necessarily) to have done so by reference to a floating rate calculated by reference to the local equivalent of LIBOR – in Paris for example this was PIBOR (the Paris Interbank Offered Rate).

Price sources

Two main Euro rates have emerged for the Euro: EURIBOR and Euro LIBOR.

(1) The London-based British Bankers Association Euro LIBOR rate is a measure of the cost in the London market based on the offered rates quoted by 16 of the most active banks in the London market.

(2) The Europe-wide EURIBOR rate is a measure of the cost of Euro funds over the Euro zone based on a panel of around 57 banks

(including at least one from each participating Member State of the Euro zone).

At the time of writing market practice is evolving as to which rates replace old rates but the general position seems to be that Euro LIBOR replaces LIBOR and EURIBOR replaces local rates such as PIBOR.

Again, it may have been necessary to amend affected contracts to which you are a party prior to EMU.

Banking days and business days

As a general rule, finance documentation utilises the concept of a "banking" or "business" day for certain purposes – the main idea being that certain obligations, such as repayment obligations and certain mechanical provisions, such as rate setting, should only be required to be performed or achieved on a working day for all concerned. Definitions of business or banking day contained in contracts in existence on 1 January 1999 may need to be changed to reflect and dovetail with a new reference rate, such as Euro LIBOR or EURIBOR, since Euro business days will be based on those days on which the Euro clearing system or "TARGET" is operational. TARGET stands for the TransEuropean Automated Real Time Cross Settlement Express Transfer System and TARGET operational days are different from business days which existed in relation to the old national currency units pre-EMU, the principal difference being that bank holidays will not be excluded from the definition. A TARGET business day will be any weekday, except Christmas Day and New Year's Day, when they fall on a weekday.

In view of the definition of a TARGET day, companies based in the United Kingdom agreeing to change a definition of business or banking day in all existing contracts should bear in mind which provisions and therefore, which events will require them to be in the office and operational. Any definition should ensure that whilst all business days or banking days (or other term) as defined are also TARGET days, not all TARGET days are business days or banking days (or other relevant term) for the purposes of the document in question.

Interest calculation basis

As a general rule the calculation of interest under financial agreements is done according to certain market conventions relating to the currency in question in payment. For example, the calculation of interest accruing on a principal amount denominated in Belgian francs was calculated according to market convention for a given period according to the actual number of days elapsed, assuming a year of 365 days. Sterling shares the 365-day year convention as did the escudo and Irish pound. The convention applicable to the Euro is 360 days.

No prohibition/no compulsion principle - difficulties

As has been mentioned above, a debtor may, at any time during the transitional period, elect to discharge a payment denominated in a national currency unit by payment in Euro. Likewise, the right would accrue to a lender of a loan to advance a sum in Euro instead of the national currency unit in which the loan is denominated.

Clearly, this may be problematical for a debtor who in the absence of a right to terminate the relevant contract will have to go through the administrative burden of converting the Euros received into the desired national currency unit

2.6 Conclusion

The extent to which the Euro impacts on a company based in the United Kingdom will depend ultimately on the circumstances and business unique to the company in question. The message for companies is that despite the United Kingdom remaining outside the Euro zone, it is likely that, sooner or later, companies in the United Kingdom will nevertheless be required to transact business in the Euro and will therefore, have to recognise and deal with the impact of this in their contractual banking and funding arrangements.

Appendix

Glossary of terms

"convergence criteria"	the economic and other criteria that a member of the European Union must meet before it may elect to adopt the Euro as its currency and participate in the third stage of European Economic and Monetary Union
"day E"	the day on which Euro notes and coins are to be introduced into circulation in the participating Member States of the first wave. At the time of writing this is to be 1 January 2000
"EMU"	European Economic and Monetary Union
the "Euro zone"	those countries which are members of the European Union and participants in the Euro. At the time of writing they are: Germany, the Netherlands, Italy, France, Ireland, Austria, Spain, Portugal, Belgium, Luxembourg and Finland
the "final stage"	the period commencing on E day and ending on the day on which national currency units cease to be legal tender in their relevant Member States. At the time of writing this is to be 1 July 2002 in respect of the participants in the first wave
the "first wave"	the adoption of the Euro by Germany, France, the Netherlands, Austria, Belgium, Italy, Spain, Portugal, Ireland, Finland and Luxembourg on 1 January 1999
the "third stage"	the third stage of European Economic and Monetary Union, namely the adoption of the Euro as a single currency
"triangulation"	the three-stage process whereby, prior to 1 July 2002, an amount of Euro denominated in one national currency unit of a participant State is converted into its equivalent in the national currency unit of another participant. For example, a conversion of 100 French francs into Dutch guilders.
the "transition period" or "transition phase"	the period commencing on 1 January 1999 and ending on E day

*Chapter 3**

· Rounding Rules ·

3.1 Introduction

The aim of this chapter is to discuss the rounding rules which are used to govern the convergence rate between the Euro and the national currencies which make up the so called National Currency Units (NCUs) in the transitional period.

The issue of rounding has always been important in currency conversion. Historically, this issue has been dealt with by economic operators. However, the advent of the Euro required fixed legal rules for dealing with rounding because the Euro NCUs are converted by the application of a legally fixed conversion rate rather than by relying on an exchange rate fixed by the market.

On 1 January 1999 the Euro became the currency of the 11 participating Member States pursuant to Article 2 of Council Regulation (EC) 1103/97. The Euro is denominated in units of one Euro. A Euro is divided into 100 cents. This means that in respect of payments or accounting practices monetary amounts will have to be rounded to the nearest cent.

In the transitional period from 1 January 1999 until 31 December 2001 the Euro will be divided into NCUs (*i.e.* the current currencies of the participating Member States – French francs, Deutschmarks etc) according to the conversion rates set by Regulation 1103/97 which do not round into convenient fractions or multiples of one Euro. This means that because NCUs are legally the equivalent of Euros the conversion between NCUs and Euros has to be treated differently from normal foreign exchange transactions between Euros and foreign currencies (*e.g.* US dollars).

3.2 Legal rules governing rounding

Articles 4 and 5 of Regulation 1103/97 set out the rules on rounding. These Articles form part of the *lex monetae* of the EU Member States

---

* This chapter was written by Mike Pullen, Associate, Dibb Lupton Alsop, Brussels.

that have adopted the Euro. Article 4 sets the rules for the use of the conversion rates (Article 4(1) to (4)). Article 5 deals with how monetary amounts based on the application of the conversion rules should be rounded.

The provisions of Article 5 apply exclusively to conversions from NCUs to Euros, and from Euros to NCUs. The rounding rules do not interfere with other rounding rules or practices used in areas, such as foreign exchange where the rules will be applicable only to the extent that a conversion between NCUs and Euros is involved in the transaction. Furthermore, rounding rules which apply internally within a Member State, such as rules governing the calculation of interest or fees, are not governed by the rounding rules under Article 5 and national practices will continue to apply.

3.3 Application of the rounding rules

Use of the conversion rates

Article 4(1) of Regulation 1103/97 states that the conversion rates shall be defined as one Euro in relation to each of the NCUs of the participating Member States. The common version rates must have six figures (*e.g.* 1 Euro = 1.43256 NCU). When the conversion rules are applied the conversion rates must be applied exactly with six significant figures and no truncating of the conversion rate is allowed (Article 4(2)).

In making conversions from Euros to NCUs or from NCUs to Euros only the conversion rates set out under Article 4 can be used. In the case of a conversion from Euros to NCUs the amount expressed in Euros has to be multiplied by the conversion rate. On the other hand, in conversions from NCUs to Euros the NCUs will have to be divided by the conversion rate.

Article 5 sets out the rules governing the rounding of monetary amounts which results from the application of the conversion rate. The general rule is that amounts converted into Euro from NCU use have to be rounded to the nearest cent before being paid or accounted for

However, in dealing with rounding from Euros to NCUs the rules have an amount of flexibility to take into account the different situations in the Member States. Conversions from Euros into NCUs should be rounded to the nearest sub-units or in the absence of the sub-units nearest unit of a particular NCU in accordance with national law and practice. For example, a conversion into Belgian francs would be rounded to the nearest centime, this being the lowest sub-unit amount in the Belgian currency but it is the Belgian national practice to round from one Belgian franc to the next Belgian franc in complete units. In cases such as this the national practice is allowed to stand and rounding to the nearest sub-unit is not required.

No bilateral rates have been fixed for rounding between NCUs. This is because any attempt to fix the rates would result in minor inconsistencies. This in turn, would give rise to the possibility of arbitrage currency speculation. In order to avoid this situation Article 4(4)) sets out the following rule for the conversion of one NCU into another.

The monetary amounts denominated in one NCU have to be converted into Euros and then converted from Euros into the target NCU. The amount which results from the intermediate transfers into Euros may be rounded to not less than three decimal places. However, it should be noted that the Regulation imposes a minimum level of accuracy for the intermediate result in Euros. This means that in certain cases more than three decimal places may be used in the intermediate conversion into Euros resulting in small discrepancies in the final monetary amounts as expressed in the target NCU.

How are the rounding rules applied under Article 5?

The rules set out in Article 5 of Regulation 1103/97 are only applicable after a conversion (*i.e.* the multiplication or division of the initial currency amounts by the conversion rate). Any other operation is outside the ambit of Article 5. Moreover, the rules set out under Article 5 are only applicable to monetary amounts "to be paid or accounted for".

The term "monetary amounts to be paid" encompasses all forms of monetary obligations. These obligations are required to be rounded to the nearest cent when converted from an NCU or to the nearest fraction or multiple of the NCU when converted from Euros. Once a conversion has been made, rounding must take place before a payment is executed, *i.e.* at the time when the monetary amount to be paid is computed with the intention of making the payment.

The term "monetary amounts to be accounted for" covers amounts which are used to value tangible assets, amounts contained in legislative provisions and offers of sale. Theoretically, the same rounding rules apply to "monetary amounts to be accounted for" as apply to "monetary amounts to be paid" pursuant to the provisions of Article 5.

However, in respect of monetary amounts to be accounted for these rules should be treated as a minimum standard of rounding accuracy, *i.e.* it is the lowest level of rounding in accuracy that is allowed under the Regulation. This can be seen in recital 11 of the Regulation which points to the use of rounding practices, conventions or national provisions which provide a higher degree of accuracy for intermediate computations.

When dealing with certain market sectors it may be necessary to round converted amounts with a much greater degree of accuracy than to the nearest cent - for example, in the case of sales offers which contain prices including a fraction of the smallest sub-unit of an NCU such as offers on the sale of food in supermarkets. Therefore, a dual price display which gives the Euro price incorporating a fraction of a cent in order to obtain a greater degree of accuracy is compatible with the provisions of Article 5.

Application of rounding rules to conversions and reconversions into the original NCU

Transactions involving the conversions of monetary amounts from Euros to NCUs may occur in payment systems when a number of financial intermediaries are engaged in the processing of payments and where accounts to be credited or debited are in different currency denominations.

Article 4(3) of the Regulation provides that the same conversion rate shall be used for conversion as between the Euro and NCUs and between NCUs and Euros. This has the effect of limiting any possible rounding differences that may arise by introducing uniform conversion rates for either way transactions. However, implementation of this Article cannot exclude rounding differences altogether because the value of the smallest unit of a particular NCU may not be equal to the value of the smallest Euro unit (the cent).

As mentioned above, the rounding rules contained in Regulation 1103/97 constitute part of the *lex monetae* of the EU and they are applicable to conversions involving both NCUs and the Euro. Transactions which take place before or after the conversion operations stipulated in the Regulation fall outside the rounding rules. Therefore, rounding of monetary amounts to be converted outside the provisions of the Regulation are governed by either legislative or contractual provisions which are outside the scope of *lex monetae* (*e.g.* national tax legislation authorising tax payers to round the monetary amounts in their tax returns to the nearest unit of an NCU rather than a sub-unit will fall outside the scope of the Regulation). Furthermore, this option will continue to be valid for tax payers in respect of conversions made including amounts which are computed as a result of a conversion between an NCU and Euros).

Declaration of small amounts

In cases where the amounts to be rounded are very small, rounding to the nearest cent for each individual item may lead to large rounding discrepancies. This problem can be addressed by either rounding the items together as a job lot, *i.e.* using the price of 100 pieces of any item as the basis for rounding rather than the price of individual items or alternatively by expressing the value attributed to each individual item with more than two decimals.

3.4 Conversion between NCUs and third country currencies

Conversion between the Euro and third currencies, such as the US dollar, falls outside the scope of the rounding rules set by Regulation 1103/97. Therefore, the rounding rules to be applied to such transactions are governed by the rules of contract law or market convention. However, given the fact that there is unlikely to be an officially set exchange rate between NCUs and third country currencies after the entry into force of the third stage of the Euro programme it is likely that the rounding rules set out in the Regulation will need to be applied after 1 January 2002. For example, the conversion of an amount of US dollars into French francs would require that the US dollars first be converted into Euros by applying the US dollar/Euro exchange rate. The Euro amount would then be converted into French francs by using the conversion rate and the rounding rules set out in the Regulation.

However, in the case of the transfer from French francs into US dollars the amounts would first be converted into Euros by applying the Euro/NCU conversion rate but Article 5 of the Regulation would not be relevant because the intermediate computation of the amount from the NCU the Euro would not need to be rounded. This is because the final step of the transaction is to convert the Euro amount into US dollars and the final step of calculating the amount in US dollars is not covered by the Regulation.

3.5 **Conclusion**

The rounding rules offer a uniform (if somewhat complex) model for the conversion of NCUs into Euros. The aim of the rules is to ensure the smooth transition of the third stage of the Euro programme on 1 January 2002. Whether or not this goal is achieved remains to be seen.

*Chapter 4**

Redenomination of Share Capital

4.1 Introduction

Redenomination is the term used by which the nominal value of a share is restated in another currency, such as the Euro, rather than, say, in sterling without affecting in a material way the nominal value of the share.

Whether or not the United Kingdom joins the single currency, many companies may choose to issue shares denominated in Euro or redenominate their existing share capital into Euro (as well as trade non-Euro denominated shares in Euro which is not dealt with here). Should the United Kingdom decide to participate in the single currency, all UK companies which have a share capital will need to consider the effect on their share capital, preferably at an early stage, rather than waiting until the end of any transitional period (which would be no more than three years from the date of entry into the single currency) when automatic conversion from sterling denominated shares to shares denominated in Euro could cause possible difficulties, for instance, because of rounding adjustments.

The UK Government issued a consultation paper in January 1998, "The Euro: Redenomination of Share Capital", and is to issue a further consultation paper. This was to have been before the end of March 1999 but is not now likely to occur before the end of 1999. This will contain a draft Order detailing a simplified procedure which can be followed by UK companies wishing to redenominate their share capital into Euro or other non-sterling currency. The Order will also address other related company law issues.

The following is based on the 1998 consultation paper, a statement issued by the Minister of State for Trade and Competitiveness in Europe in September 1998 following that consultation exercise, and subsequent discussions with the Department of Trade and Industry. It should be

* This chapter was written by Julia Stout, Partner, Dibb Lupton Alsop.

noted that the final picture may differ although it is not expected to change to any material extent.

4.2 The present position

Key company law provisions which need to be looked at in the context of the Euro are:

- the present requirement for public companies to have a minimum authorised share capital denominated in sterling;
- the current ability of companies to denominate shares in a "foreign" currency;
- the current ability of companies to redenominate their share capital;
- current procedures for altering share capital.

Minimum share capital

Private companies may have any amount of authorised share capital. No minimum is actually prescribed by legislation although such a company must have at least one member who must have at least one share of a stated fixed amount, however small; this does not need to be a whole number. The maximum authorised share capital is laid down in a company's memorandum of association. This can be altered by an ordinary resolution of shareholders.[1]

Whilst the maximum for a public company is also laid down in its memorandum of association, under the Companies Act 1985[2], a public company must have a minimum authorised and issued share capital of £50,000 denominated in sterling. This accords with the EC Second Company Law Directive which requires public companies to have a **minimum** share capital of not less than 25,000 ECU (which roughly equated to £50,000 when the provisions of the Companies Act 1985 implementing the Directive were brought into force). It was said, in the *Scandinavian Bank* case[3], that the Directive appeared to require this amount to be denominated in the national currency of the Member State in which the company is incorporated (*i.e.* sterling in the case of a

---

1 Companies Act 1985, s 121.
2 *Ibid*, ss 11, 117 and 118.
3 *Re Scandinavian Bank Plc* [1987] 2 WLR 752.

UK company). However, the point was not directly at issue in the case. Nor does the Directive expressly state this; it merely prescribes how (since the ECU was not a currency in itself) the equivalent in national currency should be calculated so that an argument that the minimum amount could be expressed in any national currency (provided that it equated to 25,000 ECU) was considered to be equally valid.

In any event, from 1 January 1999, the Euro replaced the ECU for the purposes of all EU legislation (including the Second Company Law Directive). This put beyond doubt the ability of all Member States (including the UK) to provide for the minimum capital requirement for a public company to be denominated either in Euro or in its national currency. As far as other non-Euro, non-sterling currencies are concerned, the European Commission has now confirmed that the Second Company Law Directive will allow the minimum capital requirement to be denominated in any legal currency. In the United Kingdom, the Companies Act 1985 will have to be amended to allow for redenomination in a non-sterling currency, including the Euro.

Denomination of share capital

The *Scandinavian Bank* case made it clear that (subject (in the opinion of the court) to the requirement for a public company to have £50,000 share capital denominated in sterling) companies may denominate their share capital, or different parts of their share capital, in a currency, or in several different currencies, other than sterling (subject to shareholder authority).

No problem arises for newly incorporated **private** companies denominating all their share capital in Euro or other non-sterling currency; nor for newly incorporated public companies denominating their share capital above £50,000 in a non-sterling currency (and all their share capital if the proposed amendment to the Companies Act, mentioned above, is made); and nor for existing companies issuing new shares in a non-sterling currency (whether or not their existing share capital is expressed in sterling or otherwise). The problem, however, arises where companies wish to **redenominate** their existing share capital.

Redenomination of share capital

Companies can already change or reorganise their share capital using procedures laid down in the Companies Act 1985 (see below). These procedures could be used for redenominating share capital. However, because they are not specifically designed for this purpose, the process is rather convoluted which means that it can be costly and time consuming.

Regardless of the currency into which shares are redenominated, a conversion at a specified exchange rate is unlikely to result in a whole number: for example, the exact Euro-equivalent amount of a share with a nominal value expressed, say, in sterling may need to be stated to a very great number of decimal points which may cause difficulties, for instance in the accounts.

The Council Regulations on the Euro[4] (the relevant provisions of which the UK Government believes will apply to share capital and its denomination) provide for conversions to Euro to be rounded to the nearest cent. Redenomination of sterling share capital to Euro in accordance with the Regulations, therefore, is likely to affect in a small way the nominal value of the shares because of this rounding.

Since the nominal value is not relevant to the price at which a share trades, a change in the currency in which the nominal value is expressed will have no effect on the actual investment price of the share. There may, however, be problems from a company law perspective. If the rounding causes the overall value of share capital to increase, there will be a problem if this brings the value above the authorised share capital of a company; if the rounding causes a decrease, it could bring the share capital below the minimum for a public company and, for all companies, could amount to an unlawful reduction in share capital.

For UK companies which have part of their share capital denominated in the currency of a participating Member State – in francs, guilders or Deutschemarks, for instance – redenomination is a more immediate issue. During the transitional period (until 31 December 2001), a "no compulsion/no prohibition" regime operates so that there is no obligation to redenominate; but, at the end of the transitional period, currencies of participating Member States will cease to exist. This means that, unless those UK companies with share capital denominated in the currency of a participating Member State have redenominated that share capital to Euro (or another legal currency) during the transitional period, there will be an automatic redenomination at the end of the transitional period to the Euro. Such companies are advised to take action before this occurs.

---

4 See Chap 1.

Alteration of share capital

Provided that a company is authorised by its articles of association and shareholder approval is obtained, the Companies Act 1985 already includes procedures for changing or reorganising share capital in a number of different ways, some of which could be used or adapted for redenominating shares:

- The authorised share capital can be increased.[5] The new shares created could, in theory, be denominated in Euro if valuation and accounting issues could be dealt with satisfactorily.
- The authorised share capital can be consolidated into shares of a larger nominal value or sub-divided into shares of a smaller nominal value.[6] This could help to achieve a whole number nominal value of each share following a conversion of sterling denominated to Euro denominated shares.
- Any authorised share capital not issued can be cancelled, thereby reducing **authorised** share capital.[7]
- **Issued** share capital can be reduced. This requires authority in the articles of association, a special resolution of the shareholders and the approval of the court.[8-9] The existing share capital (denominated, say, in sterling) would be cancelled and new shares could be issued denominated in a non-sterling currency, such as the Euro (subject, as has already been mentioned, to a public company having £50,000 share capital in sterling, until the appropriate amendment has been made to the Companies Act 1985).

  One problem in using the reduction of capital procedure for effecting redenomination is deciding on the conversion rate which should apply. If it is to be the exchange rate on the day the court approves the reduction, the shareholders will not know of the rate when they vote on the special resolution. If it is to be the exchange rate on the day the shareholders vote on the special resolution, any significant fluctuation in the rate between then and the day the court hears the petition for reduction could, in extreme cases, lead to the court not giving the necessary approval because it may consider it unfair to

---

5 Companies Act 1985, s 121(2)(a).
6 *Ibid*, s 121(2)(b) and (d).
7 *Ibid*, s 121(2)(e).
8-9 *Ibid*, s 135.

shareholders in the circumstances; the court in reduction of capital issues is particularly concerned that all material facts are brought to the attention of the shareholders and that they are notified of any material changes before the court confirms the reduction.[10]

- The company could buy back its own (issued) shares[11] (or redeem any redeemable shares). This does not need court approval. There should be express provision in the articles of association. An ordinary resolution of shareholders is needed for a purchase on a recognised investment exchange;[12] a special resolution is needed for an off-market purchase.[13] The shares are cancelled on purchase.[14] This procedure can give rise to tax and stamp duty issues.

  A public company can only use the proceeds of a fresh issue of shares (which has been made solely for the purpose of the buyback) or distributable reserves[15] if it chooses to buy back its own shares; a private company can, in addition to these two sources of "funding", use its capital.[16] Where a fresh issue of shares has been made for the purpose of the buyback, the new shares issued could be denominated in Euro (provided there is sufficient authorised share capital expressed in Euro). Where distributable reserves are used, an amount equal to the nominal value of the shares bought back (which, as mentioned above, have to be cancelled on purchase) has to be transferred to the capital redemption reserve.[17] This reserve could then be used to make a bonus issue of Euro-denominated shares. The capital redemption reserve, representing as it would the nominal value of existing sterling shares bought back, will be expressed in sterling so that conversion rate uncertainties could cause problems.

- The company could defer all its existing shares into valueless deferred shares to be bought back in due course for a nominal amount. On deferment, new shares denominated in Euro (or in another currency) could be issued to shareholders by way of a

---

10 *Re Jessel Trust* [1985] BCLC 119.
11 Companies Act 1985, ss 162-181.
12 *Ibid*, s 166.
13 *Ibid*, s 164.
14 *Ibid*, s 160(4).
15 *Ibid*, s 160(1).
16 *Ibid*, s 171.
17 *Ibid*, s 170.

bonus issue provided there were sufficient reserves which could be capitalised for this purpose and subject to both the articles of association and there being sufficient authorised share capital expressed in Euro (or other currency). This does not involve any court confirmation but can be complicated.

The Companies Act does contain a further possible mechanism which might be more appropriate for redenominating share capital to Euro (but only in respect of paid up shares).[18] This was not considered in the January 1998 consultation paper. A company is permitted to convert all or any of its paid-up shares into stock and re-convert that stock into paid-up shares of any denomination. There would need to be an express power in the articles of association in order to convert; Table A which forms the basis of most companies' articles of association does not contain such a power. Also, although this would not need court approval because the monetary amount of shares or stock remains unchanged, the procedure is not entirely straightforward because companies cannot issue stock direct.

The Department of Trade and Industry is of the view that the Companies Act does not give any authority for changing the **currency** of the stock or shares in the course of a process of division, sub-division or conversion.

Further tax complications can arise using any of the methods, and particularly stamp duty on the repurchase of shares where that procedure is used. The Department of Trade and Industry has been asked to consider discussing with H M Treasury the possibility of introducing an exemption from stamp duty for this purpose.

It is clear that, as has been mentioned previously, whilst existing procedures could be used, none are easily adopted for redenominating existing share capital.

4.3 The advent of the Euro

As mentioned elsewhere in this work[19], the Euro became a reality on 1 January 1999. Just to recap, two EC Council Regulations lie behind the Euro. The UK Government has stated that, although these Regulations do not specifically mention shares and share capital, it

18 *Ibid*, s 121(2)(c).
19 See Chap 1.

believes that they will apply to share capital and its denomination where relevant.

The first Regulation (1103/97) deals with, amongst other matters, the replacement of the ECU by the Euro, conversion rates and rounding rules. It applies to all Member States, including the United Kingdom. The second Regulation (974/98) includes provisions for substituting the Euro for the national currencies of participating Member States. This does not apply directly to the United Kingdom (until and unless, of course, the UK decides to join the single currency). However, its provisions are likely to be recognised in the United Kingdom as a matter of international law.

4.4 The proposed legislation

The UK Government had intended to issue a second consultation paper on the redenomination of share capital in March 1999. The final picture may differ from the following as and when that consultation paper (which is likely to contain draft regulations) is issued.

Whilst the position is not entirely clear, chiefly because the United Kingdom is not currently a participant in the single currency and it is not at all certain that it will be in the foreseeable future, the Government appears to be plotting a course which will allow for the necessary alteration to share capital with the minimum of procedural requirements, whether or not the United Kingdom decides to join. At the same time, proposed amendments will allow for redenomination of share capital into any other non-sterling, non-Euro currency.

The Government has taken the view that legislation should be introduced now to facilitate redenomination. This will enable all companies to time any decision on redenomination well ahead of the United Kingdom's entry into the single currency (if this should occur) in the most cost effective way; for instance, shareholder approval could be obtained in the ordinary course of an annual general meeting rather than it being necessary to call an extraordinary meeting solely for this purpose. It will also make it easier for those UK companies which have some part of their share capital denominated in the currency of a participating Member State to redenominate ahead of automatic conversion to the Euro on 1 January 2002.

It is understood that a new, simple procedure for redenominating share capital into the Euro or other foreign currencies is to be introduced which broadly is likely to deal with the following:

- nominal values to be redenominated by resolution;
- the conversion rate which would apply;
- how companies should convert and round nominal share capital;
- how companies should treat changes in nominal share capital arising solely as a result of denomination;
- whether shareholders or the directors should authorise a resolution on redenomination;
- the denomination of the minimum authorised capital of public companies.

Appropriate amendments to the Companies Act 1985 are likely to be made under the Deregulation and Contracting Out Act 1994. This effectively allows a "short cut" procedure for amending primary legislation. It was hoped that the amendments would be in place by the end of 1999, but this is clearly not now likely.

It should be noted that companies will not be obliged to use the new procedure for redenominating their share capital. They will still have the option of using existing Companies Act procedures. Another important point to note is that, at no time, will there be any compulsion to redenominate. At the end of the transitional period (if the UK decides to participate in the single currency), conversion will take place automatically (although, as already mentioned, companies may find it preferable to take positive action in advance of automatic conversion).

Importantly, there is likely to be specific provision in the legislation to protect the rights of shareholders and relevant third parties: where either group has rights linked to the nominal value of the share, the new procedure could not be used in any way which altered those rights without the consent of **all** those affected.

Redenomination by resolution

Companies may be able to resolve that any reference to share capital denominated in one currency in any legal document (such as a company's memorandum and articles of association) should be taken as a reference to the equivalent amount in Euro or other legal currency. At the time of writing, no details are available so that it is difficult to know how this will work in practice. A perceived problem in legislating for this in respect of any legal document is that it could cause complications, for instance, where there are unpaid calls on shares or where there are references to shares denominated in a particular currency in subscription agreements or options.

It was suggested in the January 1998 paper that the authority to redenominate could either be by resolution of the shareholders or by board resolution.

A number of options were proposed:

- an ordinary resolution of each class of shareholders;
- a board resolution with shareholders being given the opportunity to challenge the decision. This is how the transition from "manual" to electronic trading was dealt with when "paperless" share trading through Crest was introduced;
- an ordinary resolution of each class of shareholders whilst the United Kingdom remains outside of the single currency and a board resolution if the United Kingdom decided to participate (with shareholders being given the right to challenge this even though conversion would be automatic at the end of a transitional period).

The UK Government has announced that the legislation will provide that an ordinary resolution will be required to redenominate existing share capital while the United Kingdom remains outside the single currency. During the transitional period, the authority to redenominate existing share capital into Euro denominated share capital can be given by board resolution, although shareholders will be able to challenge the directors' decision. In any event, redenomination will occur automatically at the end of the transitional period.

An ordinary resolution will be needed to redenominate existing share capital into a currency other than the Euro, whether the United Kingdom remains out or goes into the single currency. There will be no provision for this to be effected by board resolution.

The conversion rate

If the United Kingdom joins the single currency, the rate of conversion between the Euro and sterling will be fixed.

A number of options were put forward in the January 1998 consultation paper as to how to determine the conversion rate before the United Kingdom joins. The question was also asked as to whether legislation should deal with this matter at all.

A particular rate quoted on a particular market on a particular day

There has been much debate on what day could be specified as the "particular" day. Similar considerations apply as were mentioned in relation to a reduction of capital under existing legislation. If the "day" is a day before redenomination becomes effective (*e.g.* the day the relevant resolution is passed), fluctuations in exchange rates between then and the day redenomination becomes effective could mean that the value on that day may be very different from the actual value on conversion. If the "day" is the day redenomination becomes effective, the value will not be known when the authority to convert is given.

An average rate over a period

The majority of respondents to the January 1998 consultation paper agreed that legislation should prescribe the method for determining the conversion rate to avoid confusion but felt that the rules should be as flexible as possible so that companies could be left to a certain extent to choose what best suited them. It is understood that the rules will prescribe a range of dates from which a choice could be made (*e.g.* the rate prevailing on any day within a specified period in advance of the conversion day) or an average over a period. Whatever date is chosen, the resolution for redenomination could specify that, if fluctuation in the exchange rate between sterling and the currency into which the share capital is to be converted is greater than a specified percentage, the resolution will not take effect. It is not thought that the draft Order will prescribe for this but it is something which companies could consider doing.

The level of conversion

Two proposals were put forward:

(1) Conversion should apply to each individual share rather than total nominal share capital.

(2) Conversion should apply to total nominal share capital.

If conversion were to take place at the level of each individual share, the value of the total nominal share capital would be the converted amount of each share multiplied by the number of shares in issue. If rounding is applied, converting each individual share is likely to produce a greater difference between the sterling-stated amount of total nominal share capital and the Euro-stated (or other non-sterling) amount than if conversion takes place at the level of total nominal share capital. Also, where conversion takes place at the individual share level, rounding could lead to shares which currently have a very small nominal value (perhaps fractions of a penny) being rounded down to nil!

A third possibility was suggested: that companies be left to choose the level at which they wanted conversion to take place rather than it being prescribed in legislation. It was noted that, whichever level of conversion were chosen, the **number** of shares in issue would not change.

It is understood that the draft Order will provide for conversion at the level of total nominal value of each class of share capital rather than at the level of each individual share, thus minimising any differences which rounding may produce.

Rounding

If the United Kingdom were to participate in the single currency, the rounding rules in the second of the relevant EU Regulations would apply to a conversion from sterling to the Euro. This means rounding to the nearest Euro cent, that is, to two decimal places of Euro.

However, whilst the United Kingdom remains out of the single currency and in relation to conversions to currencies other then the Euro, companies could have been left to choose whether to round converted values or not. However, the Department of Trade and Industry has accepted the majority of views of those who responded to the January 1998 consultation that legislation should be introduced to provide a clear framework and clear rules. Where redenomination is carried out following the procedure laid down in the Companies Act 1985 as amended, companies will have to round the converted amount (of total share capital) to the nearest legal unit or sub-unit of the currency concerned, if this is the Euro, the position will be the same as if the relevant EU Regulation applied, that is, to the nearest Euro cent.

If redenomination is carried out using a procedure other than that laid down for this purpose in the amended Companies Act 1985 (for instance, if companies wanted to redenominate ahead of the proposed legislation coming into force), it is thought that companies could choose to round or not (or, indeed, could choose the level at which they wished to convert).

The Second Company Law Directive requires shareholders' approval for any adjustment to share capital, however small. Rounding is likely to produce such an adjustment. However, the Department of Trade and Industry has taken the view that the Directive applies in this respect to an economic change only. Rounding converted total share capital would merely produce an adjustment by a very small fraction. This would not represent an economic change. Therefore, the legislation could, and is likely to, provide that conversion and rounding in accordance with the laid down procedures will not require shareholder approval.

Legislation is also likely to provide that court approval will not be needed where redenomination causes a reduction in capital. There is some precedent for this: where public companies are obliged to cancel shares forfeited or surrendered to the company on failure to pay for those shares and reduce share capital on the nominal amount of those shares, directors can do this without getting court confirmation and without a special resolution being passed.[20-21]

The individual nominal value of each share will be calculated by dividing the converted and rounded amount of total share capital by the number of shares. This is likely to result in the nominal value for each share being expressed to a number of decimal places. Although companies could choose to leave the nominal value at that, they may wish to **renominalise** the nominal value of each share, that is, alter the nominal value of a share to produce a whole number rather than an amount expressed to one or more decimal places.

It is thought that legislation will be introduced to allow companies to renominalise (where renominalisation is carried out in conjunction with redenomination) without court approval provided that the company's other undistributable reserves are adjusted by a corresponding amount and shareholder approval is obtained. Where renominalisation results in an increase in share capital, an ordinary resolution would be needed. Where a decrease in share capital results, a special resolution would be required in accordance with the Second Company Law Directive.

20-21 Companies Act 1985, s 147(1).

Minimum share capital

The Companies Act 1985[22] is to be amended to allow for the minimum authorised share capital of public companies to be stated in any legal currency. Further provision will be made so as to ensure that fluctuations in the rate of exchange between sterling and other currencies do not bring the value of non-sterling denominated share capital significantly below the £50,000 sterling authorised minimum.

The Companies Act will also be amended to provide that any reduction in capital below the minimum authorised amount for public companies caused by rounding down on redenomination to Euro will not be taken as a breach of the minimum share capital provisions of the Companies Act provided that the conversion and rounding follow prescribed rules.

No par value shares

The 1998 consultation paper discussed the possibility of companies issuing shares which had no nominal or par value at all as a way of simplifying redenomination. This would dispense with the need to consider rounding and conversion issues.

Where share capital has a true no par value, the total proceeds of a share issue are shown as capital rather than the nominal value being shown as capital and any premium over the nominal amount being shown in a share premium account. The total proceeds from any share issue would be undistributable. (It is to be questioned whether this would be more stringent than at present when the share premium account can be used, albeit in a very limited way.)

It is pointed out that the EC Second Company Law Directive does allow, in a limited way no par value shares broadly based on how such shares are dealt with in Belgium. The system requires an amount to be established for accounting purposes, an "accountable par". This would effectively be little different to the position in the United Kingdom now and would not provide any easier a mechanism for redenominating shares than the proposed legislative changes.

Since providing for a true no par value share would require amendments not only to the Companies Act 1985 but also to the EC Second Company Law Directive, the matter is not to be dealt with at present.

---

22 *Ibid*, s 118.

4.5 Impact of redenomination on ancillary areas

As previously mentioned, the legislation will provide that, where shareholders or third parties have rights linked to the nominal value of the share, the new procedure laid down for redenominating and renominalising share capital could not be used in a way which altered those rights unless **all** shareholders affected consented.

Share certificates

Where the prescribed procedure for redenomination is followed, the Department of Trade and Industry believes that neither the Companies Act 1985 nor any Stock Exchange rule would require a company to reissue share certificates showing the newly denominated nominal value of the shares represented by the certificate; this is in contrast to the position if the company cancelled or repurchased existing shares and issued new shares, in which case new share certificates would have to be issued (unless the shares were held in dematerialised form).

There is a precedent for this. When sterling was decimalised in 1971 there was no requirement to issue new share certificates.

A company's articles of association may specify that the certificate should show on its face the amount paid up on the shares represented by the certificate; or the certificate might show the sterling stated nominal value because it is part of the "name" of the class of shares, for example "1p Ordinary Shares". It is thought that such considerations will be covered by the ability of companies to resolve that reference in any legal document to the denomination of a share in a national currency will be treated as a reference to the appropriate amount of Euro or other legal currency.

If share capital is renominalised, the number of shares will change so that it is likely that certificates will have to be replaced.

Dividends

Dividends can now be paid in any currency, subject to a company's articles of association. Whilst the United Kingdom remains out of the single currency, dividends on sterling shares are likely to be paid in sterling. This may also be true even though the shares themselves may have been redenominated into a non-sterling currency.

If the United Kingdom joins the single currency, dividends could be paid during the transitional period either in sterling or Euro but, if a shareholder had a sterling account, any payment in Euro would have to be converted by the bank or building society into sterling before being credited to the shareholder's account. At the end of any transitional period, dividends previously paid in sterling would have to be paid in Euro as sterling will have been superseded by the Euro as a currency.

This is not likely to be a problem for most ordinary shares. However, difficulties may arise in relation to certain types of shares, for instance, preference and interest bearing shares, where the dividend is a percentage of the nominal amount of the share or is a fixed monetary amount. Redenomination of such shares involves similar problems to those of redenominating bonds.[23]

Where dividends are now paid in the currency of a participating Member State, payment can continue to be made in that currency until 1 January 2002 when the Euro will automatically supersede it. Payment could, of course, be made in the Euro during this time.

Redeemable shares

Conversion and rounding adjustments could affect the amount payable on redemption where this is stated to be a fixed amount.

Convertible shares

It is hoped that legislation will be introduced to enable conversion of shares from one class to another to take place without the complications currently foreseen where shares of one denomination are converted to shares of a different denomination. It is thought that provision will be made to the effect that any differences which arise on conversion in these circumstances would be transferred to the equivalent of the capital redemption reserve, a generally undistributable reserve.

Nil or partly paid shares

Where shares are nil or partly paid, a shareholder has an obligation to pay up the amount outstanding on the share. Applying rounding rules

23 See Chap 2.

to the amount outstanding could mean that a shareholder may have a greater or lesser obligation where the shares are redenominated.

Whilst it may have little effect in practice, it should be mentioned that, where dividends are expressed as a percentage of the amount paid up on a particular share, the entitlement could change if the nominal amount of the share changed because of conversion and rounding.

Class rights

Conversion and rounding applied to different classes of shares could alter the holdings of each class relative to each other class. Even if this is only by a small amount, it might amount to a variation of class rights requiring the separate approval of each class affected. It is understood that the legislation will provide that rounding in accordance with the new procedure for redenomination will not amount to a variation of class rights unless the rights specifically provide that it should.

It is not known whether this will also be the case in respect of redenomination of monetary amounts in the share rights. Examples of this include a dividend entitlement expressed as a monetary amount, a redemption or other return of capital entitlement expressed as a monetary amount or involving a formula, part of which is a monetary amount, a voting right expressed in terms of a monetary amount (*e.g.* one vote for every £1 in nominal amount of shares held), or a ratio for conversion into another class of shares which is expressed as a monetary amount. It is thought that these examples will amount to a variation of class rights – and the legislation will not prescribe otherwise. Shareholder consent will, therefore, be required.

The legislation is expected to deal with the conversion of one class of shares into another.

Adjustments to reserves

Where rounding leads to a change in value of total nominal share capital, there would need to be a corresponding adjustment to reserves:

- the amount of any decrease would have to be transferred to an undistributable reserve;
- the amount of an increase would need to be debited to a "distributable" reserve, such as the profit and loss account.

Other miscellaneous matters

- Voting rights should not be adversely affected as a result of redenomination. It is not known how rights expressed in terms of a monetary amount, *e.g.* one vote for each £1 share, will be dealt with.
- Where a company redenominates its share capital, the number of issued shares should not change so that relative holdings will remain the same. Renominalisation may alter the number of existing shares.
- Holders will not be obliged to sell any part of their holding.
- The legislation will not affect the ability of a company to denominate its shares in a non-sterling, non-Euro currency or to issue, trade or account for shares in such a currency.
- Filing: any alteration in share capital has to be notified to the Registrar of Companies within one month.[24] It is not thought that this currently includes notifying redenomination of share capital. It is not known whether the legislation will amend the provisions to include redenomination.

4.6 Conclusion

The proposed new procedure will greatly simplify a company's redenomination of its share capital into any legal currency. Where prescribed procedures are followed, court approval will not be needed. Depending on when the authority to redenominate is given, either a board resolution or a shareholder resolution will be required (unless redenomination is into a non-sterling currency other than the Euro in which case a shareholder resolution will always be needed).

Whilst companies will be able to use existing Companies Act procedures to effect redenomination, unless their needs are pressing, they should be advised to await the new Companies Act procedures.

---

24 Companies Act 1985, ss 122 and 123.

*Chapter 5**

· Tax Issues ·

5.1 Introduction

Despite the United Kingdom not being one of the "in" countries when the Euro was introduced on 1 January 1999, there are a number of tax issues which UK companies will have to consider as a result of the first phase of the single currency coming into force. These issues are of a technical nature. The purpose of this chapter is to provide an overview of them, and where relevant, compare how the United Kingdom intends to deal with them and the tax treatment which will be adopted by some of its EU partners who are part of the "in" crowd.

Unlike most of its other EU partners, the United Kingdom was given a choice whether or not to join the single currency on 1 January 1999. Various statements made to Parliament by the Chancellor of the Exchequer clarified the UK Government's position on the Euro. Whilst the UK Government has said it is in favour of the United Kingdom joining the Euro, it will not do so until the economy is ready to join. It is now clear that the United Kingdom will not join EMU and the Euro within the life of this Parliament, but will, subject to the result of a referendum, join at a later date. Despite this "wait and see" policy, a number of technical changes were required to both UK company and taxation laws.

The areas of concern for tax payers that are within the charge to UK taxation are generally as follows:

(1) The conversion/transition to the Euro will inevitably lead to additional cost for business. What will be the tax consequences of this enforced expenditure?

(2) What impact will the Euro have on a tax payer's transfer pricing policy?

(3) How does the Euro affect the already highly technical treasury function of multinational groups?

(4) What are the administrative considerations?

---

* This chapter was written by Trevor James, Partner, Dibb Lupton Alsop.

5.2 Costs incurred by UK companies on introduction of Euro

It is clear that if and when the United Kingdom joins the single currency, all UK businesses will be affected. However, many businesses experienced the wind of change from 1 January 1999. The single currency is not only changing the method of trading for some UK businesses, but also its commercial behaviour. For example, a UK business which has a factory or trading outlet in another EU State, or UK resident companies who import and/or export in the EU will be directly affected by the single currency. Similarly, businesses that trade in the financial markets, which already deal in a multiplicity of foreign currency, have already felt the impact of the single currency. A UK subsidiary of a multinational group is likely to be required by its parent to trade in the single currency, for commercial, administrative and reporting reasons. The effect of monetary union will also in some cases have an impact on purely domestic trade. A UK resident supplier, for example, who supplies goods or services to a UK subsidiary of a multinational group may be required to bill the customer in Euro. Such companies were prepared for the introduction of the single currency (and will have to prepare further if and when the UK itself joins the Euro). Failure to do so may not only result in a loss of commercial advantage but may result in the total loss of business.

Preparing for the Euro

In July 1997, the Chancellor of the Exchequer, Gordon Brown announced the formation of the Business Advisory Group on EMU. The purpose of the Group was to consider in detail, the practical questions arising from the introduction of the single currency. The report emphasised the importance for all businesses of gearing up to meet the challenges of the single currency. It would be impossible to set out all of the changes that were required to prepare for the single currency. This primarily depended on the size and nature of the business in question and the sector in which it operates. However, a number of preparatory steps and changes were likely to be common to most businesses. These can be briefly stated as follows:

- instructing management consultants to provide strategic advice on the changes required to adapt to the single currency;

- staff training;
- production of new price list and marketing material;
- marketing initiatives to make customers aware of the new pricing;
- the development and modification of computer systems and software;
- the modification of equipment used by traders, for example tills, vending machines and ATMs;
- legal due diligence of major contractual relationships to assess the impact of the single currency;
- modification of accounting systems and policies for reporting in the Euro.

Having incurred all of these costs (and undoubtedly more), an important point that must be addressed is whether the tax payer will be able to claim a deduction in relation to these costs when calculating its liability for corporation or income tax.

Some concern was expressed by the Institute of Chartered Accountants of England & Wales (ICAEW) tax faculty on the tax treatment of conversion cost and in response, the Inland Revenue confirmed that it was sympathetic with the faculty's view. However, notwithstanding this sentiment, the Chancellor did not deem it necessary to introduce new provisions to deal with the deductibility of conversion cost. As a result of this, general principles must be used to determine to what extent such cost will be allowable.

Qualifying for tax deductions

There are a number of hurdles which a UK tax payer must get over to successfully claim a deduction in relation to an item of expenditure.

In relation to traders, it must first be shown that the expenditure in question was of a revenue rather than a capital nature. There are a number of cases, in which this concept and distinction have been considered at great length. In one case, a one-off payment to get rid of an onerous provision in a lease was held to be of a capital nature and was therefore not deductible. In another case, a banking subsidiary of the tax paying company was insolvent, and to prevent the tax paying company itself going into liquidation, it was forced to participate in a rescue plan, which required an injection of £50 million into the banking subsidiary. The tax paying company then claimed a deduction in respect of this payment which was allowed. There are a number of tests which the courts use to determine whether expenditure is capital or income. One is the so called "once and for all test", that is whether an expenditure is made only once and without a reoccurring nature. Another test is the "enduring benefit" test, that is "when an expenditure is made, not only once and for all, but with a view to bringing into existence an asset or an advantage for the enduring benefit of the trade". The distinction is in some cases very hard to determine, and it is sometimes made even more difficult where there is a lack of symmetry between a payment in the hands of the recipient and in those of the payer, that is a capital payment may become a revenue payment or vice versa.

Assuming that the tax payer is able to get over the capital/income hurdle, the next point that must be proved is that the item of expenditure falls within the statutory provision which determines what is an allowable expenditure. This is to be found in section 74 of the Income and Corporation Taxes Act 1988 (Taxes Act 1988). Briefly, section 74 provides that any disbursement or expense will not be deductible when calculating a tax payer's profits unless that expenditure has been incurred wholly and exclusively for the purpose of the trade. It follows that if there is any duality of purpose, that expenditure will not in theory be deductible, (although in practice an Inspector of Taxes may allow the expenditure to the extent that it has been incurred wholly and exclusively for the purpose of the trade, in which case, difficult questions of apportionment may arise). Finally, the tax payer must show that the expenditure in question is not specifically barred by legislation from being tax deductible, for example, client entertainment.

At one end of the scale, a tax payer should be able to claim a tax deduction for expenditure incurred on staff training and marketing without any dispute from the Tax Inspector. As regards the cost of converting computer software, the Inland Revenue published a press release in 1998, stating that cost incurred purely to convert software to deal with the single currency is unlikely to be capital and will therefore be deductible. However, the press release goes on to say that where costs are incurred, for example, to upgrade as part of a strategic overhaul, such expenditure will be of a capital nature and will therefore not be deductible. The press release does not deal with the situation where a lump sum is spent for both conversion and upgrade. Whilst one would expect the Inland Revenue to take a commercial approach and allow the tax payer to apportion the expenditure, the prudent approach is to separate the cost at the outset and identify the amount incurred for conversion (and hence deductible) and the amount attributable to the upgrading of the system, which will be capital and not deductible. Most businesses will be familiar with this issue as a result of the expenditure incurred on the millennium bug problem.

Difficulties arise in relation to expenditure incurred to modify capital equipment. For example, what will be the position in relation to the cost incurred on adapting coin operated vending machines if the United Kingdom joins the single currency? Such expenditure will be of a capital nature. The Inland Revenue has not to date confirmed what the tax treatment of such expenditure will be. However, one hopes that the attitude taken will be in accordance with the sympathetic views expressed in response to the ICAEW's tax faculty's paper.

If expenditure is held not to be deductible, all may not be lost. If such expenditure is incurred on the acquisition of equipment which falls within the definition of "plant and machinery" for capital allowances purposes, the tax payer will be entitled to claim a form of tax depreciation equal to 25% of the reducing balance of the asset. The allowance is reduced to 6% where the asset in question is a "long life asset", that is an asset which has a useful economic life of at least 25 years.

Having reviewed the position in the United Kingdom on conversion cost, what will be the position in other Member States?

Conversion costs in other Member States

In the Netherlands, it has recently been announced by the Dutch Ministry of Finance that special rules are to be introduced aimed at small and medium size businesses to assist in the cost of conversion to the single currency. In essence, such costs will be deductible from taxable profits in the year that the expenditure is incurred. In Denmark, conversion costs may under local tax laws be treated as current costs or restructuring costs and will therefore be deductible. This also applies to costs incurred on software conversion and modification. The French tax authorities published an instruction telling firms how to take expenditure linked to conversion into account when calculating taxable profits. Under these instructions, the items of expenditure that will qualify for a deduction will be very limited and restricted and therefore major expenditure on items such as the modification of computer equipment will be capital and therefore not deductible.

It would appear that the United Kingdom is not out of line with its EU partners and in some cases offers a more favourable treatment.

5.3 Transfer pricing

It is perhaps fair to say that in recent years transfer pricing has become the most important issue in the international tax world. Transfer pricing is the setting of prices at which a company engages in cross border transactions in goods, services and intangibles with parties with whom they are associated. Traditionally, a company's transfer pricing policy will be designed to minimise the group's worldwide taxable profits. The objective will therefore be to have profits taxed in low tax jurisdictions and have expenses relieved in high tax jurisdictions. The globalisation of the market place and the growth of electronic commerce have lead to an increase in the practice of transfer pricing.

The issue of transfer pricing is by no means new. The work and research undertaken by the Organisation for the Economic Co-operation and Development (OECD) is substantial, which includes a set of guidelines for its members as to how to deal with transfer pricing issues. The OECD model tax convention (which is the framework for tax treaties between trading countries), sets out the general basis of how pricing should be determined between associated parties. Article 9 provides:

> "Where a Contracting State includes in the profits of an enterprise of that State – and taxes accordingly – profits on which an enterprise of the other Contracting State has been charged to tax in the other State and the profits so included are profits which would have accrued to the enterprise of the first-mentioned State if the conditions made between the two enterprises had been those which would have been made between independent enterprises, then that other State shall make an appropriate adjustment to the amount of the tax charged therein on those profits."

Whilst the language used in this article is difficult in places, the meaning of the article is clear; the profits subject to tax in one State should be calculated on the basis of tax payers acting on an arm's length basis. There are similar concepts in relation to the articles dealing with interest and royalty payments between connected persons.

New rules on transfer pricing

The Finance Act 1998 introduced a new modern transfer pricing regime in the United Kingdom. The new regime takes effect from the start of a company's accounting period ending on or after 1 July 1999. Therefore, all companies whose accounting period commenced on or after 2 July 1998 will (assuming the accounting period is not shortened) be within the regime.

The new rules are designed to put them within the self-assessment regime (hence the dates for the two coinciding) and are given teeth by an interest and penalty regime which may in theory run from the date the tax payment was due. The penalty can potentially be up to 100% of the tax on the transfer pricing adjustment. These rules are therefore of a mandatory nature, since the tax payer will have to confirm, by signing the tax return, that the profits have been computed on an arm's length basis.

As one would expect, because the rules are essentially concerned with tax avoidance, the provisions are very widely drawn and bring the United Kingdom rules in line with Article 9 referred to above and the OECD transfer pricing guidelines. Generally, the new rules can apply to transactions where one party controls the other or where there is a joint venture company in circumstances where a person has a 40% interest in the joint venture vehicle. (The joint venture provisions only apply where two shareholders or partners control the company or partnership and each has a 40% interest in the company or partnership.) As to what constitutes control for these purposes, the definition covers cases where a person is able to control a company as a result of holding shares in the company, by voting-power, or by any other power conferred by the articles of association or other document regulating the affairs of the company.

As mentioned above, one of the essential features of the new regime is that the obligation is placed on the tax payer to ensure that its pricing accords with the arm's length policy. The tax payer is required to maintain and keep detailed documents to justify its pricing policy.

The introduction of the single currency will remove what was one of the important defence shields from the transfer pricing defence armoury, that is the justification of different pricing because of exchange rate fluctuations. The introduction of the Euro will increase price transparency and will enable the Inland Revenue to make a more accurate inter-company comparison. This will inevitably increase the pressure on companies to implement a pricing policy, which will withstand any scrutiny of the Inland Revenue. Tax payers are well advised to embark on this exercise sooner rather than later and ensure that the necessary supporting documentation is in place. Otherwise, there will be a serious exposure of incurring substantial penalties and interest.

It is not uncommon for multinational groups to arrange their funding in such a way to benefit from the different rates of tax in the various jurisdictions in which it operates. This is done by focusing on the worldwide tax rate of the group as a whole and where funding is required in a high tax jurisdiction, there will be an incentive to do this by means of debt rather than equity, so that the borrower obtains a deduction in respect of the interest paid on the debt. Traditionally, the coupon on the debt will be determined by a number of factors, one of which will include the currency risk that the lender will assume. On the introduction of the single currency, this consideration will disappear where lending is between companies resident in countries that are part of monetary union. One consequence of this may be that the tax authorities may pay greater attention to the level of interest being charged intra-group to determine whether there is any transfer pricing within the group.

The issue of transfer pricing may also arise where a group treasury strategy includes the use of cash pools around a group. Under this arrangement, one subsidiary may be in credit and another overdrawn. This could be viewed as the former providing the latter with an interest-free loan. Since the pool is now likely to be in a single currency, the arrangement will become more apparent and tax authorities may require an appropriate adjustment to take into account the interest which would have been charged had the parties been acting at arm's length.

5.4 Foreign exchange legislation

As a result of a line of cases in the late 1980s and early 1990s, the Finance Act 1993 introduced a new regime for foreign exchange gains and losses. As a result of this legislation, for accounting periods that began on or after 23 March 1995, new rules apply to the determination, and charge or relief of exchange gains and losses. These rules apply to most forms of companies.

The exchange gains and losses rules are of a very technical nature, the detail of which is beyond the scope of this book. However, the important features of the legislation are as follows:

(1) Exchange gains and losses in respect of certain assets and liabilities and forward currency contracts are recognised as they accrue between set translation times.

(2) Trading exchange gains and losses are treated as trading items. Net non-trading exchange gains are assessed under Schedule D, Case VI. Special rules apply for the relief of net non-trading exchange losses.

(3) Certain unrealised exchange gains on long term capital items may be deferred.

(4) Exchange differences are generally calculated in sterling, although trading profits or losses may in certain circumstances be calculated in non-sterling currencies.

Following discussions with the Bank of England and certain other representative bodies, the Chancellor of the Exchequer issued a press release announcing how the UK Government proposed to deal with the technical issues arising from the introduction of the single currency. Legislation was subsequently introduced in the Finance Act 1998. There was general agreement that these changes dealt adequately with the issues. The remaining part of this section will briefly discuss the issues and the changes.

Finance Act 1998 changes

Where a company conducts and accounts for its trade (or part of it) in a foreign currency, subject to satisfying certain conditions, the foreign exchange legislation allows the company to make an election to adopt a currency other than sterling as its functional currency. Changes were made to the law to treat the Euro as a foreign currency for these purposes. Therefore, where there is an election in place which allows the taxpaying company to compute its tax computations in a currency of a country which has adopted the Euro, *e.g.* French francs, the election will be deemed to convert automatically into a Euro election for the first accounting period ending after 1 January 1999, when the company prepares its first accounts in Euro.

If an election is in place for a non-participating currency, *e.g.* the Japanese yen, the changes introduced in the last Finance Act, will enable a company to re-elect for the Euro, assuming that the normal conditions for election are satisfied. Such a re-election will be effective from the beginning of the next accounting period after it is received. Therefore, the election must be made before the start of the first accounting period to which the company wants the election to apply.

As mentioned above, unrealised exchange gains on debt, which are considered "long term capital assets or liabilities" may be deferred. There was some concern that if the assets or liabilities are redenominated in such a way as to appear to give rise to a different asset or liability, the deferred gain or loss would be considered to be realised and therefore ineligible for deferral. However, the Chancellor made it clear that it was not the UK Government's intention that redenomination should result in the deferral being lost and introduced legislation to prevent this.

There is also a provision in the legislation that enables a company to elect to hedge a foreign currency asset with a foreign currency liability or currency contract. Where an election is made, exchange movements on an eligible liability or currency contract may be deferred. As above, the matching will not be affected by the redenomination of either the asset or the liability.

The legislation contains a number of anti-avoidance provisions which may be applied where the Inland Revenue considers that one of the main benefits of an asset or liability is the accrual of a loss or where a transaction is entered into otherwise than at arm's length. Some concern was expressed that where the conversion of assets or liabilities occurs, or the main economic purpose of the transaction has fallen away as a result of the introduction of the single currency, the anti-avoidance provisions will be evoked. The Chancellor confirmed, however, that the introduction of the single currency will not in itself result in the anti-avoidance provisions applying, provided "the Board believes that no abuse is taking place".

As mentioned above, these provisions are very complex and detailed and the above is merely a summary of the main changes.

5.5 Administration

It has already been mentioned that a UK company can elect to adopt the Euro as its accounting currency. A company can also pay its corporation tax, PAYE and National Insurance in Euro. The Government has already announced that it will bear the cost of translation in sterling. If payment is made in Euro, the tax payer will be credited with paying the sterling equivalent translated at the value date when the funds are received. However, if there is a change in the exchange rate between sterling and the Euro between the date the payment is sent and the date that it is credited, this may result in either an overpayment or underpayment of tax, depending on the direction of the movement. Any exchange rate risk is that of the tax payer not the Government. Tax payers are therefore advised that if they decide to make payments of tax in Euro, the preferred method of payment should be by electronic funds transfer rather than by cheque.

The VAT position is not as straightforward. Where a UK resident company prices its product in Euro, it will still be obliged under UK VAT law to include an amount in sterling. There is an implication that since the VAT amount must be stated in sterling, the VAT records must also be kept in sterling. Once the VAT amount has been expressed on the invoice, the exchange rate is fixed. Therefore, if there is a movement in the rate between the date of the invoice and the date of payment, the risk will be on the tax payer, unless it is able to shift the risk onto the customer.

The intention was that the introduction of the single currency should be tax neutral. This was of course an ideal position. However, it is fair to say that as far as the United Kingdom is concerned, the Government has gone a long way to achieve this objective.

*Chapter 6**

· Pensions ·

6.1 Introduction

There is a whiff of complacency in the pensions world as far as European Monetary Union is concerned. A survey conducted by the National Association of Pension Funds (NAPF) in July 1998 found that a substantial majority of UK pension scheme administrators and fund managers are assuming that the United Kingdom will join the Euro, but at the same time only one quarter of the administrators and fund managers surveyed had taken any steps to respond to the Euro. This discrepancy implies that UK pension scheme administrators and fund managers do not regard the Euro as bringing about or necessitating significant changes for UK pension schemes and that other issues, such as pension sharing on divorce and stakeholder pensions and the new pensions review of the pensions legislative framework, are regarded as being more important.

The purpose of this chapter is to demonstrate that the Euro could nevertheless have a profound impact on UK pension schemes. Clearly, the extent of the effect of the Euro will depend upon whether the United Kingdom eventually joins the Euro. The greatest effect will arise after the introduction of Euro notes and coins in circulation in January 2002 and if and when the United Kingdom does join the Euro, rather than in the transitional period leading up to that point. Whilst the United Kingdom remains outside the Euro zone, as currently, the Euro's greatest impact as far as UK pension schemes are concerned will be on those schemes which are sponsored by multinational employers, which include employees resident in Euro zone countries, such as the Republic of Ireland, as members of the scheme.

The short term and direct impact of the Euro on UK pension schemes may be limited, although it may involve additional costs for sponsoring employers of such schemes. The longer term and indirect impact may be much greater, but of its very nature is more speculative. There should be investment and funding implications for UK pension schemes from the

---

* This chapter was written by Jeremy Harrison, Partner, Dibb Lupton Alsop.

Euro, whether the United Kingdom is in or out of the Euro, but these will depend upon the economic effects which the Euro has, in particular on interest and inflation rates. If the Euro does result in reduced interest and inflation rates, which is the conventional expectation, then that would increase the real cost of most final salary/defined benefit schemes and accelerate the existing trend for new schemes, especially for smaller and medium-sized employers, to be defined contribution/money purchase schemes. It is widely expected that the Euro should add to the pressure on Member States to remove or at least relax some of their restrictions on foreign investments by pension schemes. Investments by Euro zone pension schemes within the Euro zone will, of course, no longer be foreign investments for this purpose. The Euro is also thought likely to encourage the development of pan-European pensions, in other words, pension schemes covering employers and employments across a number of Member States, although there are a number of obstacles to the development of such pensions, especially the differences which exist in the tax, social security and regulatory regimes of the various Member States.

Even whilst the United Kingdom remains outside the Euro, investments of UK pension schemes in Euro zone countries will have a reduced currency risk because of the single currency. Conversely the need for diversification of investments may require a re-categorisation of investments in Euro zone countries by reference to sector rather than country or even a reduction in the proportion of investments in Euro zone countries. If and when the United Kingdom joins the Euro, then the general expectation is that investments by UK pension funds in Euro zone countries will increase as a proportion of total investments since such investments will be regarded as being domestic investments in the home economy. The increase in investments by UK pension schemes in Euro zone countries would be at the expense of the current high proportion of UK pension scheme investments which are concentrated within the United Kingdom.

If and when the United Kingdom does join the Euro, there is an obvious impact in contributions and benefits being required to be paid in Euros from that point (assuming that it is after July 2002). Sterling will no longer be used for this purpose. Clearly, this change will need to be communicated to the affected pension scheme members. This will have a knock-on effect on scheme administration, scheme accounting and various regulatory requirements which will need to be satisfied in Euros rather than sterling.

6.2 Contributions and benefits

While the United Kingdom remains outside the Euro

In the case of a pure UK pension scheme with UK resident employee members only, there will be no change in the regulatory requirements as to the currency in which contributions and benefits are to be paid. These will still be paid in sterling. Regardless of the existence of the Euro, whilst the United Kingdom remains outside the Euro zone, UK regulatory requirements will not require contribution records, benefit statements and annual reports and accounts to be in Euros but in sterling. However, it will be open to employers to provide for their schemes to accept contributions in Euros and for schemes to show amounts in Euros on benefit statements in addition to the sterling amounts. Multinational companies trading in the Euro zone may well require UK pension providers to do this for their own administrative purposes.

Existing regulatory requirements will only require contributions and benefits to be in Euros under UK pension schemes in the case of employees resident in the Euro zone, such as in the Republic of Ireland, and only then from July 2002 when the Euro will be the only currency in the Euro zone.

If and when the United Kingdom joins the Euro

Payments and scheme records

Contributions to UK pension schemes and benefits payable from UK pension schemes will be required by law to be paid in Euros once the Euro is in circulation and if and when it replaces sterling. Should the United Kingdom join the Euro, this would take place, at the earliest, from July 2002 from which time the replacement of sterling would be complete. If the United Kingdom were to join the Euro at any time during the transitional period leading up to 2002, which is now unlikely, the currency required by UK legislation for contributions and benefits would remain sterling until the end of the transitional period. Contribution records in the transitional period would be required to be converted to Euro at the frozen rate of exchange fixed between the Euro and sterling in the year of changeover from sterling to the Euro. Benefit statements issued to scheme members and annual reports produced by scheme trustees would be required to show amounts in both currencies.

The "no compulsion/no prohibition" principle would apply were the United Kingdom to join the Euro in the transitional period, under which employers and schemes could agree for payment either in sterling or in Euros. Payments would be required to be credited in the scheme account, however, in the denomination of that account. Where payments of contributions are made by bank transfer (including direct debit or standing order), employers and members would be able to contribute to the scheme bank account either in sterling or Euros, but the scheme trustees would be required to credit the scheme bank account in the currency of the account.

Regulatory issues

Deduction of employee contributions

If and when the United Kingdom does join the Euro, changes will be required to written authorities from employees to employers to deduct employee contributions from wages under section 13 of the Employment Rights Act 1996 if the existing written authority refers to a fixed amount of sterling. An authority which so provided would have to be changed to a fixed amount of Euros. Section 13 of that Act prohibits employers from deducting employee contributions from wages or salary without a written authority from the affected employees. Failure to obtain such a written authority before making a deduction could give rise to complaints by affected employees to the industrial tribunal brought against the employer in question. This principle extends equally to deductions exceeding the terms of a written authority, for example, in the wrong currency, or in the wrong amounts, as well as deductions without any authority whatsoever.

However, where a written authority refers to deductions of a fixed percentage from wages or salary, rather than fixed amounts of currency, then clearly there will be no need to change the written authority for the purposes of section 13 of the 1996 Act on any change from sterling to the Euro.

Disclosure requirements

Regulation 4(5) of the Occupational Pension Schemes (Disclosure of Information) Regulations 1996 (SI 1996/1655) obliges UK pension scheme trustees to notify all members and beneficiaries (apart from untraceable deferred pensioners) of any change in relation to the scheme which "will result in a material alteration" in the basic information required to be provided by those Regulations, either before the change takes effect, where it is practicable to do so, or in any event not later than three months after the change has taken effect.

If and when the United Kingdom joins the Euro, and from July 2002, the requirement to pay pensions and contributions in Euros instead of in sterling would probably be regarded as a material alteration in the basic scheme information for the purposes of the 1996 Disclosure Regulations, even though the change would be a compulsory national change rather than a scheme-specific change brought about by a change in the scheme rules. The trustees would therefore be obliged to inform all active members (*i.e.* current employees who are continuing to accrue benefits under the scheme), traceable deferred pensioners (who have ceased to accrue benefits under the scheme but who retain entitlements under it) and existing pensioners of the change to payment in Euros.

Regulation 5(3) of the 1996 Disclosure Regulations provides that where the amount of the benefit payable to a person is or is about to be altered otherwise than in accordance with pension increases guaranteed by the scheme's own provisions, the changes in the amounts of benefits must be announced by the scheme trustees to the recipient of the benefit. This must be done as a matter of course (without depending upon any request from that person), before or within one month after the date on which the decision to alter the amount is made or the date (if later) from which the alteration has effect. UK pension scheme trustees will therefore be obliged to inform existing pensioners of the new amount of their pensions in Euros before or within one month after the date of change of currency of payment from sterling to Euros.

The cost of complying with the above disclosure requirements will have to be met by the scheme's sponsoring employers or from the scheme assets.

Contributions and payment schedules

Section 87 of the Pensions Act 1995 obliges the trustees of UK occupational pension schemes which are money purchase schemes to secure that there is prepared, maintained and from time to time revised, a payment schedule showing the rates of contributions payable by the employers and active members to the scheme and the due dates for payment of those contributions. Regulation 18 of the Occupational Pension Schemes (Scheme Administration) Regulations 1996 (SI 1996/1715) requires trustees of such schemes to include within the payment schedule details of amounts payable towards the scheme by the employer in respect of expenses likely to be incurred in the following scheme year, together with due dates for payment of those expenses.

Section 58 of the Pensions Act 1995 obliges the trustees of UK final salary occupational pension schemes to secure that there is prepared, maintained and from time to time revised, a schedule of contributions showing the rates of contributions payable by employers and active members to the scheme and the due dates for payment of those contributions. In the case of this schedule, the contributions payable by the employer are to be the contributions adequate for the purposes of satisfying the statutory minimum funding requirement under sections 56 to 61 of the 1995 Act and must therefore be certified by the actuary to the scheme.

If and when the United Kingdom joins the Euro, and from July 2002, trustees of UK occupational pension schemes would be obliged to revise their payment schedules (in the case of money purchase schemes) and schedules of contributions (in the case of final salary schemes) to show Euro values in place of sterling, at least where fixed amounts of currency are shown in the schedules. Again, as with written authorities for deductions of employee contributions from wages (see above), where the relevant schedules show fixed percentages of pensionable salary or earnings, then the change in currency of payment from sterling to Euros will make no difference to the relevant schedule.

Inland Revenue limits

UK occupational pension schemes can only be treated as approved by the Inland Revenue as exempt approved retirement benefit schemes under Chapter I of Part XIV of the Income and Corporation Taxes Act 1988 and so gain the attendant tax advantages, such as tax-free retirement lump sums, tax-free investment growth (apart from dividends on UK shares) and tax-free contributions, if the Inland Revenue's limits on benefits payable from and contributions payable to the scheme are complied with. Scheme members who joined a scheme after 1 June 1989 are subject to the earnings cap on their remuneration (including benefits in kind) which can be taken into account for the purposes of such benefits and contributions. This earnings cap began at £60,000 per annum in 1989 and, subject to one exception, has been increased each year in line with the UK Government's General Index of Retail Prices since that date, so that it now amounts to £87,600 per annum (for the tax year 1998 to 1999).

For a member who joined a scheme after 16 March 1987 and before 1 June 1989, a similar limit of £100,000 per annum applies to the final remuneration which can be taken into account for certain of his benefits.

Certain other Inland Revenue limits are expressed in terms of a fixed amount of sterling. Retained lump sum death benefits of no more than £2,500 may be disregarded for the purposes of calculating the limit applicable on such death benefits. The triviality limit, *i.e.* the maximum amount of aggregate pension which may be entirely commuted (*i.e.* exchanged) for a retirement lump sum, without there being exceptional circumstances of serious ill health on the part of the relevant recipient, is currently £260 per annum.

All of the above fixed amount limits would be required to be converted to Euros if and when the United Kingdom joins the Euro or from July 2002 if later. In all probability there would be statutes and regulations prior to the United Kingdom's entry giving effect to the relevant conversions and stating the new amounts in Euros, but it is arguable that the very act of the United Kingdom joining the Euro would, in the absence of any such express statutory provision, provide overriding authority for schemes to apply a Euro limit rather than a sterling limit.

6.3 Administration issues

UK pension scheme administrators will be faced with the need to convert historic administration records into Euros from sterling should the United Kingdom join the Euro. This will already affect UK pension schemes prior to any UK entry into the single currency as far as concerns members of a scheme who are resident in the Euro zone. Pensions in payment in respect of Euro zone residents will need to be converted immediately into Euros at the end of the transitional period in July 2002, rounded to six figures. Euro zone residents retiring after the end of the transitional period will need to have their final pensionable salary figures re-based into Euros for the purposes of the calculation of their scheme benefits in the case of final salary schemes and in any event, for the purpose of calculating Inland Revenue limits for all UK occupational schemes. Annual benefit statements issued as of course for active members of money purchase schemes and benefit statements and transfer value quotations issued on request to scheme leavers after the introduction of the Euro in circulation in January 2002 will be required to be converted to Euros for Euro zone residents.

There will be pressure from multinational employers on scheme administrators to present both sterling and Euro figures during the transitional period prior to 2002 in benefit statements and transfer value quotations in respect of Euro zone residents, because of the substantial systems upgrades required to achieve the changes.

In order to minimise accounting and administration work, it would be desirable for pension schemes to switch to the Euro, as far as benefit statements and transfer value quotations for Euro zone residents are concerned, at the scheme annual renewal date or the scheme year end, rather than at any other date during the year.

Should the United Kingdom join the Euro or in the case in any event of UK pension schemes with Euro zone members, scheme administrators will be faced with the need to effect computer programming changes to recognise the existence of two currencies for the purposes of paying pensions and issuing benefit statements and transfer value quotations.

6.4 Accounting issues

Little change would occur in UK pension scheme accounts whilst the United Kingdom remains outside the single currency. Assets held by UK pension schemes in Euro zone countries have in the case of shares been re-denominated as a result of the conversion weekend at the end of 1998 and the process of re-denomination will gradually cover other asset classes such as debts issued by Euro zone governments. Assets in Euro zone countries will probably not, however, change in value merely as a result of the introduction of the Euro.

If and when the United Kingdom does join the Euro, however, on a change of the currency for the purposes of scheme administration from sterling to Euros at the scheme year end, the previous year's figures would need to be restated for the purposes of the scheme accounts from sterling to Euros.

Once it is certain that the United Kingdom is to join the single currency, it would be advisable for scheme trustees to require scheme investment managers to begin giving the trustees their regular reports on scheme investment performance in both sterling and Euros, even during the transitional period prior to January 2002, although the scheme trustees would not be obliged to have reports in Euros until January 2002 or any later date of UK entry.

It is clear from the above discussion of the administration and accounting issues that any conversion of scheme administration and/or scheme accounts from sterling to Euros in whole or in part needs to be co-ordinated between scheme trustees, scheme employers, scheme administrators and scheme investment managers.

6.5 Continuity of contracts

This issue, which is discussed in more detail in Chapter 7 may affect in particular investment management agreements made by UK pension schemes and hedging contracts protecting schemes against currency risks to which UK pension schemes or their delegates are party. Where such agreements are concerned with investments in assets in Euro zone countries, they are likely to require payments to be made in one or more of the "legacy" national currencies which are to be succeeded by the Euro. Concern has been raised as to whether the change in currency could render payment obligations impossible to perform or make performance of payment obligations radically different from those envisaged by the contract. In other words, the contract would be "frustrated".

Most investment management agreements and hedging contracts involving UK pension schemes are governed by English law, under which it is unlikely that a mere change of currency in the payment obligation would frustrate the contract. However, it is possible that provisions in the particular agreements might overturn the continuity presumption. It will be necessary in all cases for those provisions to be checked to ensure that there are no special provisions overturning that presumption.

Even where such agreements are not governed by English law, the European Commission's Article 235 (new Article 308) Regulation requires continuity of contract in the case of contracts governed by laws of Member States of the EU and makes it unlikely that the Euro would frustrate or terminate contracts governed by such laws. Generally speaking, in the case of contracts governed by laws of non-Member States, one state will recognise the currency of another and give effect to changes in it. See Chapter 7, for details of outstanding problems on continuity of contracts occasioned by the Euro.

6.6 Measures of inflation

The UK Government's General Index of Retail Prices is the measure of inflation which is most widely used by UK pension schemes for the purposes of calculating pensions increases required by legislation and required or allowed for under scheme rules and for Inland Revenue limits purposes. The Inland Revenue allows tax-approved occupational pension schemes in the United Kingdom to increase pensions in payment by the greater of either a flat 3% per annum or the rate of increase in the UK Government's General Index of Retail Prices.

The General Index of Retail Prices has been criticised as a measure of inflation for pensions purposes because it includes mortgage interest which is volatile and not of widespread relevance to existing pensioners. It also includes local authority and indirect taxes.

There are varying methods of measuring inflation within the EU. Attempts have been made to produce an EU-wide consumer price index. In 1996 interim indices were put forward which would exclude 20% of the items in the UK Government's General Index of Retail Prices, especially housing and insurance. The latest harmonised indices include all the items in the United Kingdom's index but the indices are constructed differently from that index in terms of the weightings given to individual items.

It is conceivable that the introduction of the Euro may have the effect of there being two different EU indices, one for Euro zone countries and the other for non-Euro zone Member States. However, there is no proposal to require the United Kingdom's General Index of Retail Prices to fall in line with any EU index. The introduction of the single currency does not, of course, mean that there will be uniform inflation within even the Euro zone countries. On current proposals it would still be open to the UK Government to retain a separate UK measure of inflation, which would still be used as the basis for Inland Revenue limits and pension increases under UK pension schemes.

All current actual and proposed indices for inflation arguably overstate the true rate of inflation by not reflecting improvements in quality introduced without a change in price or substitution of interchangeable commodities. The weightings in current indices are not sufficiently flexible to allow for the fact that when some commodities increase in price, consumers tend to switch to other interchangeable commodities, so that a lower proportion of the former commodity is purchased and a higher proportion of the latter.

If the General Index of Retail Prices, or any other index used, were changed so as not to overstate inflation in these ways, then the index would be reduced relative to the actual rate of inflation. This would mean a greater real rate of interest on the basis of the new index and an increased yield on index-linked stocks. Index-linked benefits would therefore be cheaper. The overall effect might be to reduce the cost of UK pension scheme funding, although there would be a greater risk of deflation, which, as discussed below, paradoxically would be likely to increase that funding cost.

6.7 Economic effects

The Euro has conventionally been thought likely to result in lower inflation and interest rates within the Euro zone and even within the main trading partners of the Euro zone countries. By the process of "Euro-creep", competitive pressures are thought likely to force down prices within the single currency/single market environment. Those countries which are thought most likely to benefit from lower inflation and lower interest rates as a result of the Euro, are those which historically have experienced higher than average inflation, such as the United Kingdom.

What effect would there be on UK occupational pension schemes if UK inflation were to be reduced say to a medium term average of 2% per annum with occasional deflation and only very infrequently inflation above 5% per annum, following a similar pattern to German historic inflation? This would involve some increases in pension costs. Paradoxically, if this were to happen, the present value of future pension liabilities would be greater and this would be even more so if there were to be a shift in scheme investments from shares to bonds. This shift might well occur as part of a trend in the United Kingdom towards a more European way of investing, and also if there were to be lower share capital growth and lower dividends on UK shares.

Lower interest rates would mean higher annuity costs, which means that the cost of purchasing a given level of pension would increase. This would be offset only in part by the lower cost of securing inflation-proofing of pensions if inflation is lower. Fixed pension increases, for example, of 3% per annum, which is allowed by current Inland Revenue limits, would become relatively more costly.

Final salary schemes with retirement pensions based on average unadjusted pay over one or three or five years would become relatively more costly, as the benefits would be based upon a higher proportion of salary at retirement. The salary in years prior to retirement would be increased by a lower rate of salary increase to arrive at the final figure, in line with lower rates of inflation.

Money purchase underpins would become more costly. These arise where scheme members are promised a defined formula for calculation of their retirement pension based on final salary, but are also guaranteed to receive at least the pension which can be provided from a money purchase account held on their behalf consisting of the contributions made in respect of them plus a fixed rate of interest. The fixed rate of interest would necessarily be a fixed low rate. In a low inflation environment, that fixed low rate would become higher relative to inflation.

Conversely, the higher annuity costs in a low inflation/low interest rate environment might bring pressure for better commutation rates for scheme members, so that they could draw a higher tax free retirement lump sum in exchange for a given amount of pension, on the basis that higher annuity costs would reduce the amount of pension which they would get from a given amount of capital.

Lower inflation rates would bring a greater risk of deflation. This would also increase the cost of funding UK occupational pension schemes. UK trust law will not generally allow trustees to agree a reduction in accrued pension rights. Section 67 of the Pensions Act 1995 prevents any retrospective amendments affecting accrued pension rights or entitlements without either the consent in writing of the affected members or an actuarial certificate that the effect would not be prejudicial to those rights and entitlements.

Accordingly, it would not be possible for UK pension schemes to reduce accrued rights even though prices would be falling and so the real cost of providing those accrued rights would be rising. Deflation would result in real increases in pensioners' income even if pensions are nominally static. Pensions would not be reduced by the negative rate of inflation, so the real cost of providing them would increase.

Index-linked gilts would no longer be an adequate match for pension scheme liabilities, since the proceeds of those gilts would reduce.

Once deflation sets in, there could be a deflationary spiral, with an increase in the burden on the current working population of paying for more costly pensions in real terms and reductions in the real income of that working population.

If the Euro does result in lower inflation and lower interest rates, because of the increased costs on schemes and employers which this is likely to involve, the Euro may well accelerate the trend for new occupational pension schemes, especially for smaller and medium-sized employers, to be money purchase schemes, rather than final salary schemes.

6.8 Investment

Changes to statements of investment principles

Section 35 of the Pensions Act 1995 obliges the trustees of UK occupational pension schemes (other than wholly insured schemes, most small self-administered schemes and one member schemes) to secure that there is prepared, maintained and from time to time revised, a written statement of the principles governing investment decisions for the purposes of the scheme ("a statement of investment principles"). The statement must explain the trustees' policy for diversifying investments and ensuring that investments are suitable for a pension scheme and that, in the case of final salary schemes, the investments are designed to satisfy the statutory minimum funding requirement. The trustees must set out in the statement their policy as to the kinds of investments to be held, the balance between different kinds of investments, the risk, the expected return on investments and the realisation of investments. The trustees must, before the statement is prepared or revised, obtain and consider the written advice of a suitably qualified investment manager or consultant and must also consult the sponsoring employer.

Even whilst the United Kingdom remains outside the single currency, the introduction of the Euro constitutes a major change which requires the trustees of UK pension schemes at least to review their statements of investment principles. At the very least, there will be changes to the foreign currency risks associated with investments by the scheme in Euro zone countries. Even if the statement of investment principles is not ultimately changed, the trustees should consider the written advice of their investment advisers and consult the sponsoring employers as to whether there should be any changes.

As time goes by, and EU Member States join or leave the Euro, those changes in the composition of the Euro zone may also require the trustees of UK pension schemes to review their statements of investment principles.

New asset classes and investment opportunities

The conventional UK pension schemes' approach to investments has been that UK shares are the best match for the sterling liabilities which such a scheme has towards its members who are resident in the United Kingdom. It seems that while the United Kingdom remains outside the Euro, there will be little change in this general approach, although the introduction of the single currency will give rise to new substantial asset classes of potential investments and investment opportunities for UK pension schemes. UK schemes will be able to invest in Euro-denominated bonds and Euro-denominated shares in place of the participating countries' bonds and shares in the former "legacy" currencies.

The credit risk applied to government debts may replace the exchange rate as the method by which the financial markets express confidence or otherwise in the performance of the economies of Member States within the Euro zone. The government bonds of weaker economies in the Euro zone may well therefore offer attractive yields for UK pension schemes. Investments in such bonds will essentially be a matter for scheme investment managers to determine, acting on behalf of scheme trustees and seeking to obtain the best possible investment return for the scheme.

Increased investment in the Euro zone?

UK pension schemes may re-organise their investments within Euro zone countries by reference to the economic sector rather than by reference to the individual countries, in view of the fact that investments across the Euro zone would now be in the same currency and so there would no longer be any spreading of currency risk by spreading investments across Euro zone countries.

If and when the United Kingdom joins the Euro, it would seem to be inevitable that UK pension schemes would invest a substantially greater proportion of scheme assets in Euro zone countries other than the United Kingdom, treating the Euro zone as a whole, rather than just the United Kingdom, as the domestic market. There would be no exchange rate risk in so doing. The principle of matching would suggest that Euro liabilities should be matched by Euro assets. However, the notion that Euro zone shares are a single asset class is qualified by the different practices of the separate national markets within Euro zone countries, with varying liquidity, separate tax systems and different market rules.

Increased overseas investments outside the Euro zone?

UK pension schemes have traditionally, as well as having a majority of assets held in domestic shares, invested a substantial minority proportion of scheme assets in overseas markets in order to get the benefit of increased returns and reduced reliance on one economy. If and when the United Kingdom joins the single currency, Euro zone investments will no longer serve this purpose since the Euro zone will be the home market. One would therefore expect minority overseas investment portfolios to consist of a greater proportion of United States, Japan and Far East investments.

Increased investments in bonds?

If the Euro does produce greater economic stability and lower interest rates, that could increase the attractiveness to UK pension schemes of bonds as opposed to shares. UK pension schemes may shift a higher proportion of scheme assets into bonds as compared with shares. On the other hand, with the development of the single currency/single market, continental Euro zone countries may well make more share capital available in which UK pension schemes may invest. There may be some harmonisation of investment practices across a Euro zone incorporating the United Kingdom.

Cross-border investment restrictions

If the Euro results in higher annuity costs in the United Kingdom, it may be attractive for UK pension scheme trustees to purchase annuities from insurers in other Euro zone countries.

It is hoped that the introduction of the Euro will coincide with a reduction in or the elimination of existing national obstacles to cross-border investments within the Euro zone, and possibly in the EU as a whole. That would increase the investment opportunities for UK pension schemes. It would also allow continental Euro zone pension schemes to invest in the United Kingdom.

Greater cross-border investments might in due course lead to the development of pan-European pension schemes covering employees across the Euro zone, and possibly across the EU, although there are significant tax, social security and regulatory obstacles to this.

If, as a result of the Euro or otherwise, there are to be more funded pensions in the EU and larger European share capital markets, there is an opportunity for UK pension fund managers with experience in European and overseas markets to demonstrate a European-wide expertise.

6.9 Funding

Assume higher real investment return?

It is far from certain that if the Euro produces lower inflation, that will mean higher real investment return for UK pension schemes. It seems likely that no higher rate of investment return will be assumed for the purposes of funding UK pension schemes unless and until it materialises over a significant period of time. This applies to both the actuarial method and assumptions used by particular scheme actuaries for the purposes of determining the ongoing funding position of UK schemes, including allowances for future salary growth and for dividend income from UK shares, and also to the statutory minimum funding requirement under section 56 of the Pensions Act 1995, which requires UK scheme liabilities to be valued by reference to UK Government bonds and UK ordinary shares.

The actuarial methods and assumptions used for the purposes of funding UK occupational pension schemes have been traditionally cautious. One would not expect speculation, albeit conventional speculation, as to the economic effects of the Euro to result in an immediate change to those methods and assumptions. Rather it is likely that no change would be made to those methods and assumptions as a result of the Euro for several years until any presumed improvement has been proven in the market place.

The need to change the MFR

There is an argument that the statutory minimum funding requirement (MFR) provides a strong incentive for UK pension funds to reduce their Euro zone exposure at the very time when the Euro zone represents an investment opportunity for them. This is because investments outside the United Kingdom in Euro zone and other overseas markets are not currently taken into account in the MFR. Such investments therefore cause schemes making them to run the risk of failing the MFR test. This is a serious issue because if the MFR test is not satisfied by a scheme, then the sponsoring employers could be legally obliged to pay very substantial sums into the scheme in a relatively short timescale.

The counter-argument is that, quite apart from the impact of the Euro, the MFR already does not reflect the actual historical investment strategy of UK pension schemes, by underplaying the heavy reliance traditionally placed by UK pension schemes on UK shares as opposed to bonds. The best way, if it can be afforded, for UK pension schemes to ensure MFR solvency in the long term is by adequate, or more than adequate, pre-funding of scheme liabilities, so that there is a healthy MFR surplus which can be used as a cushion against fluctuations in the assumed MFR rate of return. It is only if the MFR funding position is marginal that schemes run the risk of imposing substantial immediate liabilities on sponsoring employers.

If and when the United Kingdom joins the Euro, then it would seem to be necessary for the statutory minimum funding requirement to be extended to cover Euro zone shares and gilts, so as more properly to reflect the new enlarged domestic market and likely scheme investment returns. It seems likely that the MFR would be so changed if the United Kingdom were to join the single currency. It is conceivable that the MFR might be so extended even whilst the United Kingdom remains outside the Euro, but this is unlikely, principally because of the currency risk involved, unless at least the EU rules are changed to require pension funds in Member States to have unrestricted investment powers within the EU.

*Chapter 7**

· Continuity of Contracts ·

7.1 Introduction

It is a fundamental principle of contract law that, to be enforceable, a contract must be certain. That is to say, the obligations which the parties have undertaken must be set out with sufficient clarity that each of them knows what it has to do in order to perform its side of the bargain. A corollary to this requirement is that it enables the courts to identify deficient performance by one or more of the parties and to apply the appropriate sanctions.

When an event happens during the life of a contract which has the effect of making the contract more difficult, or indeed impossible, to perform or radically changes the underlying factual matrix, uncertainty is created and this can, in certain circumstances, undermine the contract either through the operation of the doctrine of "frustration" or by activating *force majeure* or other clauses in the contract itself. The circumstances in which this can occur are described in greater detail below.

During the lead up to the introduction of the Euro, great emphasis was placed on the need to ensure that the advent of the single currency did not lead to the widespread disruption of contractual relationships and the need to ensure "continuity of contracts" was identified early on as an objective of fundamental importance.[1]

In this chapter, we shall identify some of the events which might bring the continuity of particular contracts into doubt. We shall then examine the legislative response to these perceived threats (both in the European Union and elsewhere) and, finally, summarise the practical steps that organisations and individuals can take to protect their position.

---

1 See, *e.g.* the European Commission's Green Paper of May 1995, "Practical Arrangements for the Introduction of the Single Currency."

* This chapter was written by Duncan Gillespie, Associate, Dibb Lupton Alsop.

The first task is to define exactly what is meant by the term "continuity of contracts". As various commentators have noted, there is no universally accepted definition.[2]

7.2 Contracts under threat

What contracts, then, might be under threat?

- contracts containing references to monetary amounts denominated in, or calculated with reference to, the European Currency Unit (ECU) or a national currency replaced by the Euro;
- contracts which refer to screens, indices or pricing sources which disappear during the life of the contract (*e.g.* DM – LIBOR);
- contracts involving swaps or other hedging arrangements which will be rendered meaningless by the fact that both currencies involved have been replaced by the Euro at fixed exchange rates.

Some practical examples:

(1) An American construction company has contracted to build a power station in Germany. The contract, signed in 1995, specified payment in Deutschmarks. The power station is to be completed in 2001, *i.e.* after the replacement of the DM by the Euro. The value of the Euro against the US dollar is less than that previously enjoyed by the DM. The American company is unhappy at the deterioration in its return. Should it be entitled, in the absence of agreement, to abandon the contract or insist upon its re-negotiation?

(2) A borrower in 1994 took out a long term loan denominated in Italian lira. The loan was at a fixed interest rate of 18%, reflecting economic conditions in Italy. In 1999, the lira was replaced by the Euro, and interest rates across the Euro zone, including Italy, fall to 3%. After conversion, the borrower is obliged to repay the loan in

---

2 For present purposes, we shall adopt the definition proposed by the Financial Law Panel in its report "Economic & Monetary Union – Continuity of Contracts in English Law" (January 1998), which ran as follows: "A situation in which the process of EMU, and in particular the introduction of the Euro as part of that process, does not lead, as a matter of law and without the wish of the parties to the contract to: (i) the contract terminating automatically; or (ii) one or more of the parties having the right to terminate or materially alter the terms of the contract."

Euros but the bank insists that the 18% interest rate remain effective. The borrower demands a renegotiation of the contract. Does he have the right to do so?

In the absence of legislative intervention, it could be argued that the obligation to make payment in a national currency would be impossible to perform after the replacement of that currency. It is also possible that parties locked into long term payment obligations at interest rates reflecting the volatile nature of some of the former national currencies would capitalise on such uncertainties in an effort to evade their responsibilities or at least make them less expensive.

Furthermore, with some contracts it is arguable that the entire commercial rationale of the deal has disappeared with the introduction of the Euro. Examples of this might be found in swaps or other hedging arrangements where both currencies have been replaced by the Euro.

The response to these perceived threats has been a mixture of legislative intervention and initiatives from market participants (*e.g.* the International Swaps & Derivatives Association – ISDA).

The answer to the two questions posed above is that, if the contracts are governed by English law, or the law of another EU jurisdiction, the original contractual obligations of the parties will not be affected by the introduction of the Euro (unless the contract itself provides otherwise). This chapter will focus in detail on how that situation came about.

7.3 Legal principles affecting continuity of contracts

Parties to contracts frequently enter into them on the basis of a mistaken understanding of the facts as they are at the time of entering into the contract and as they might develop in future. Many, with the benefit of hindsight, come to regret doing so. The common law has always placed a heavy emphasis on giving effect to contractual obligations freely entered into and courts are very reluctant to overturn such arrangements even when it becomes evident that one party has had very much the worse of the bargain.[3]

---

3 See *Paradine* v *Jane* (1647) Aleyn 26.

Frustration

To mitigate, to some extent, the rigour of this basic rule, English law recognises that contracts may be discharged by virtue of the doctrine of frustration where an event happens after the formation of the contract which either makes the contract impossible to perform or renders the obligation radically different to that envisaged by the parties at the outset. Similar concepts apply in other jurisdictions, for example, the German doctrine of *Wegfall der Geschäftsgrundlage* or the French *Théorie de l'imprévision.*

As with many other areas of law, there is balance to be struck between, on the one hand, ensuring that the parties to a contract do not attempt to walk away from their obligations merely because the contract has become more difficult or expensive to perform and, on the other, avoiding the injustice that might result from a strict insistence on the performance of a contract after a major change of circumstances. The doctrine of frustration is not to be invoked lightly and any party seeking to do so has a significant hurdle to overcome. For that reason, cases in which frustration has been successfully argued are relatively few and far between and often have unusual facts.

Lord Radcliffe, giving judgment in the 1956 case of *Davis Contractors Ltd* v *Fareham UDC*[4] discussed the factors which the court would take into account when faced with a claim that a particular contract had been frustrated (for reasons other than impossibility or supervening illegality):

> "... whenever the law recognised that, without default of either party, it [the contract] has become incapable of being performed because the circumstances in which performance is called for would render it a thing radically different from that which was undertaken by the contract. ... it is not hardship or inconvenience or material loss itself which calls the principle of frustration into play. There must be as well such a change in the significance of the obligation that the thing undertaken would, if performed, be a different thing from that contracted for."

A further pre-condition for the application of the doctrine of frustration is that the particular event or change in circumstances must have been unforeseen, or at least unforeseen by the parties. The reason for this is that, if the event was foreseen by the parties, but they decided not to provide for it in the contract they must have been

4 [1956] AC 696 at 729.

content that the contract should survive such an occurrence. The issue of foreseeability is, of course, a vexed one in a number of legal contexts and it is notoriously difficult to decide accurately, with the benefit of hindsight, and in the knowledge that a particular event has actually happened, whether or not it was, or should have been, foreseeable several years previously.

Particular care needs to be taken in relation to events which, although acknowledged as a theoretical possibility, were considered by both parties so unlikely as not to justify explicit treatment in the contract. In these circumstances it would be dangerous to assume that the parties actually intended that the contract would remain unchanged if this event actually occurred.

In the context of European Monetary Union, it would be difficult to argue that the advent of the single currency itself was unforeseen as it has scarcely been out of the news since the signing of the Maastricht Treaty in February 1992. However, of course, it is possible that some of the economic "fall out" of the single currency may genuinely fall into the category of an unforeseen event.

If a party to a contract can satisfy the tests for invoking the doctrine of frustration then the contract is brought to an end and both parties excused from further performance.[5] The consequences of frustration are governed both by the common law and the Law Reform (Frustrated Contracts) Act 1943, discussion of which are outside the scope of this work.

Contractual provisions which may enable contracts to be varied or terminated

Force majeure or impossibility clauses

Many contracts contain *force majeure* or impossibility clauses which excuse one or other of the parties from performance where it is rendered impossible by a subsequent event such as war, floods, act of government or other calamity. However some widely drawn *force majeure* clauses could be triggered by the introduction of the Euro and, given that Article 3 of Council Regulation (EC) 1103/97 (see below) is expressed to be subject to anything that the parties may have agreed, this could bring contracts to an end, or at least bring a delay in

---

5 See, *e.g.* *Joseph Constantine Steamship Line Ltd* v *Imperial Smelting Corporation Ltd* [1942] AC 154 at 163; *National Carriers Ltd* v *Panalpina (Northern) Ltd* [1981] 1 All ER 161.

performance. However, it is unlikely that *force majeure* clauses will be triggered in all but the most unusual of circumstances.

Increased costs clauses

"Increased costs" clauses often appear in loan documentation and allow lenders to pass on the increased costs associated with the loan to the borrower. The European Commission has expressed the opinion[6], which is, of course, not binding, that clauses which refer to changes in liquidity, reserves or similar legal requirements will not be triggered by the introduction of the Euro itself.

7.4 **The EU Regulations**

Given the concerns outlined above, the need to provide a robust legal framework for the Euro has long been recognised and the result is two Council Regulations:

(1) Council Regulation (EC) 1103/97 of 17 June 1997 on certain provisions relating to the introduction of the Euro.

(2) Council Regulation (EC) 974/98 of 3 May 1998 on the introduction of the Euro.

These Regulations are sometimes referred to as Euro Regulations I and II respectively.

Regulation 974/98 came into force on 1 January 1999 and is only directly applicable in those Member States which adopted the Euro in the first wave.[7] It deals with practical issues relating to, for example, bank notes and coins and for present purposes can largely be ignored.

Regulation 1103/97 entered into force on 20 June 1997 and derives its authority from Article 235 (new Article 308) of the Treaty. This Regulation is directly applicable in all Member States.[8] This Regulation deals with particular issues of concern to businesses and was implemented in response to representations from the financial markets in particular.

---

6 See European Commission – Euro Papers No 10, December 1997 at 11.

7 The UK and Denmark have negotiated special arrangements set out in Protocols 11 and 12 to the Treaty.

8 By virtue of Art 6 and, as such, forms part of UK law without the need for implementing domestic legislation.

Needless to say, the Regulations do not apply to jurisdictions outside the European Union.

Article 3 – continuity of contracts

It is this Regulation which enshrines the principle of continuity of contracts in the context of the Euro. Article 3 states:

> "the introduction of the Euro shall not have the effect of altering any term of a legal instrument or of discharging or excusing performance under any legal instrument, nor give a party the right unilaterally to alter or terminate such an instrument. This provision is subject to anything which the parties may have agreed."

A number of important issues arise from this deceptively simple formulation.

(1) "Legal instrument" is defined, in Article 1, as "legislative and statutory provisions, acts of administration, judicial decisions, **contracts**, unilateral legal acts, payment instruments other than bank notes and coins, and other instruments with legal effect".

Even without the concluding sweep up provision, this definition is very wide and, as can be seen, explicitly includes contracts.

(2) It must be noted that Article 3 applies only to the *introduction of the Euro* and not to the economic or other consequences which ensue. It was suggested in various quarters that the scope of the Regulation should be widened to cover those as well but it was felt that any such incursion by the European law-makers into the *lex contractus* of the Member States would be beyond their powers. As a result the general law of the jurisdiction concerned will govern specific contractual issues arising during the lifetime of the contract.

Therefore there is still the possibility that frustration or other similar doctrines could be invoked to bring contracts to an end in appropriate cases, although, no doubt, any tribunal hearing such a case would have regard to the overwhelming policy priority given to contract continuity and would be even more reluctant than usual to grant relief.

(3) Not only does Article 3 prevent a party from abandoning its contractual obligations but also from unilaterally attempting to revalue or alter the deal in response to changes in circumstances.

(4) Article 3 is expressed to be subject to any contrary agreement between the parties. Therefore normal freedom of contract rules are retained and if a contract specifically provides for the economic consequences of EMU then that provision will override the Regulation.

Article 2 – replacement of the ECU by the Euro

Although Regulation 1103/97 was designed to smooth the path for the Euro, one provision has had potentially the opposite effect, that is Article 2 which provides that:

> "Every reference in a legal instrument to the ECU ... shall be replaced by a reference to the Euro at a rate of one Euro to one ECU. References in a legal instrument to the ECU without such a definition shall be presumed, such presumption being rebuttable taking into account the intention of the parties, to be references to the ECU as referred to in Article 109 of the Treaty [new Article 111] and as defined in Regulation (EC) No 3320/94."

The significance of this provision is that, in the absence of contrary provision, it enforces one for one equivalence between two currency units which are not identical, and in some cases substantially different. The ECU was not, strictly speaking, a currency in its own right but was a compendium made up of a "basket" of European currencies whose value was calculated according to a weighted average mechanism.[9] The distinction is of more than academic interest. If the transition from the ECU to the Euro is held merely to be the replacement of one currency with another then, in keeping with the convention that *lex monetae* is a matter for the country concerned,[10] automatic continuity of contracts is assured. If, however, the same change is, on analysis, the replacement of a mere unit of account with a fully fledged currency then, quite clearly, there has been a fundamental change in the nature of any payment obligation formerly expressed in ECUs which cannot, under normal contractual principles, be enforceable in the absence of legislation or the agreement of the parties.

---

9 The value of the ECU was originally defined, in Commission Dec (ECSC) 3289/75, as follows: German mark, 0.828; £ sterling, 0.0885; French franc, 1.15; Italian lira, 109; Dutch florin, 0.286; Belgian franc, 3.66; Luxembourg franc, 0.14; Danish krone, 0.217; Irish £ , 0.0759.

10 Under such an analysis the transfer from the ECU to the Euro would be regarded in exactly the same way as the recent change in Brazil from the Cruzeihro to the Real or the decimalisation of the currency in the UK in the 1970s.

A further complication arises in the case of the so-called "private ECU" or "ECU fermé". Although, for most private contracts which refer to the ECU, the official definition of the ECU was adopted, some parties chose to define their own version using only some of the constituent currencies, applying different weightings or by defining the ECU with reference to its value at a particular date. The switch over will, in these cases, bring even more significant changes to the nature of the payment obligation. In the absence of specific provision in the contract, Article 2 will enforce parity between the private ECU and the Euro. This could, depending on the original definition of the private ECU adopted, have the result of significantly changing the economics of the contract. In this context it should be noted that the presumption imported by Article 2 is rebuttable and it is open to a party disadvantaged by its operation to adduce evidence that it does not accord with the intention of the parties – though it would face the burden of proving this.

As noted above, the Regulations are only applicable in the EU and the position with respect to the continuity of contracts subject to the laws of other jurisdictions may be different.

However, the issue has been recognised by many of the leading trading partners of the European Union which have enacted legislation intended to ensure continuity of contracts in the context of the Euro. The American states of New York[11] and Illinois[12] have implemented continuity of contract legislation and similar legislation is planned in California (see Chap 9).[13] Switzerland, Japan and Singapore have also made similar provisions. Although, in general, the position in key foreign jurisdictions appears promising, specific local legal advice should be sought where a contract is governed by laws of countries outside the EU.

Industry initiatives

A number of participants in the financial markets, among the International Swaps and Derivatives Association (ISDA) has adopted a protocol to deal with the introduction of the Euro and incorporated changes in its standard documentation to deal with EMU.[14]

11 Title 16, New York General Obligations Law.
12 815 ILL Comp State Am 617/1 *et seq* (West Supp 1997).
13 Assembly Bill No 185, 1997/98 Regular Sess (Cal 1998).
14 International Swaps and Derivatives Association Inc. EMU Protocol, 6 May 1998.

The documentation consists of a main protocol which introduces a number of amendments to the ISDA Master Agreement along with a number of annexes which each deal with one specific issue (continuity of contracts, payment netting etc). Parties to an ISDA Master Agreement signify their acceptance of the protocol by lodging a letter of adherence with ISDA indicating which of the specific annexes they wish to be bound by.

The continuity of contract provisions state that:

> "the occurrence or non occurrence of an event associated with economic or monetary union in the European Community will not have the effect of altering any term, or discharging or excluding performance under the Agreement."

An exhaustive definition of the events which are associated with economic and monetary union in the European Community is given in the clause

The ISDA continuity of contract provision is very comprehensive and, in conjunction with the Regulations, should ensure continuity of contracts in the derivatives market.

Practical steps to ensure continuity of contracts

Although potential pitfalls remain, the Regulations provide a sound basis for continuity of contracts. However, parties to contracts may well wish to make specific contractual provision. Listed below are several practical steps which companies and individuals can take to safeguard their position generally:

(1) Given that the Regulations only apply in the European Union, the first step is to ensure that contracts are made subject to a law of a Member State. This will ensure (so long as the parties do not agree otherwise) that the Euro Regulations apply.

(2) Include a continuity of contract clause in the agreement. The following simple clause might be appropriate:

> "neither party shall be excused performance of its obligations under this Agreement or be entitled to vary or terminate this Agreement by reason of the adoption by the United Kingdom of the single European currency."

Parties to agreements where the unit of currency is particularly important may wish to use a more elaborate clause, perhaps along the lines of the ISDA continuity protocol referred to previously.

It may well, of course, be the case that the parties specifically do not wish to continue to be bound by their obligations following the introduction of the Euro and, in that event, the contract should explicitly say so by the inclusion of a termination provision which can be invoked at the option of either or both of the parties.

(3) Where contracts contain reference to pricing sources which disappear entirely, or private ECU obligations which are replaced by successors which are only an approximate substitute, then the contract should contain explicit fallback provisions which set out the basis upon which the appropriate calculations are to be made.

(4) During the transition period the principle of "no compulsion/no prohibition" will apply. This could mean that companies find themselves obliged to accept payment denominated in Euros when they want to be paid in one of the national currencies or, conversely, to be paid in the national currencies when they wished to receive payment in Euros. This could, of course, be extremely inconvenient, particularly if the necessary computer system enhancements have not been completed by the receiving company. If this is likely to prove an issue, the contract should contain an explicit statement that the choice of payment currency belongs to the receiving party.

(5) Most *force majeure* clauses will not, generally, be triggered by the introduction of the Euro but some particularly widely drafted clauses might. If there is any doubt, the *force majeure* clause should be amended to state that the introduction of the Euro (or the economic consequences stemming from it) are not to be considered legitimate *force majeure* events.

(6) In loan documentation, increased cost clauses should be scrutinised to ensure that they contain adequate protection for the borrower in the event that the vendor wishes to pass on substantial additional costs. Such protection might include the right to repay the loan early or to demand a certificate substantiating the value of the additional costs imposed.

(7) The introduction of the Euro will have far reaching consequences and many of these will be unforeseeable. For that reason, contracts which are sensitive to the introduction of the Euro should not only be flexible in themselves but perhaps also be capable of variation at the instance of either of the parties. If one party feels that it is likely

to be disadvantaged then it should reserve the right to make such (reasonable) consequential amendments to the contract as may be necessary to reflect the changes in the market conditions.

(8) Where an ECU obligation is expressed in terms other than the official ECU, this should be explicitly dealt with in the contract to rebut the presumption raised by Article 2 of Regulation 1103/97.

(9) Finally, although not, strictly speaking, an issue of contract continuity itself, parties should ensure that they obtain appropriate Euro compliance warranties from their suppliers and other business partners. As with the Year 2000 issue, the introduction of the Euro could have major repercussions for computer systems, both software and hardware.

Those who purchase computer software or hardware or other devices which are affected by the unit of currency, such as coin operated vending machines, should ensure, if these are to continue in use, that the contact deals with this issue by the insertion of an appropriate warranty that the product can cope with the Euro. This is preferable to relying on the terms as to quality and fitness for the purpose implied by the Sale of Goods Act. Of course, as well as the warranty provisions, the limitation of liability clauses in any contract should be scrutinised to ensure that they do not exclude or, unduly limit, the liability of the supplier in the event of a failure on his part.

Given the number of issues raised above and the number of contracts which many organisations will have in place, a mechanistic audit of every contract would undoubtedly be an impracticable option for many companies. However, all of the issues discussed above should be borne in mind when drafting new contracts, and, in appropriate cases, changes should be negotiated to existing contracts.

7.5 Conclusion

Despite the number of issues raised above, the overall conclusion must be that, at least where English law, or the law of other jurisdictions within the European Union, is concerned continuity of contracts is assured in all but very unusual cases. This conclusion is supported by the findings of the Financial Law Panel which stated that:

> "we can identify no classes of transaction of forms of contract commonly in use in financial and commercial circles, where continuity of contracts is likely to be called into question by EMU and the consequences of the change to the Euro."[15]

This discussion of continuity of contracts concludes on that reassuring note.

---

15 Financial Law Panel, "Economic and Monetary Union Continuity of Contracts in English Law""(January 1998) at 43.

*Chapter 8**

· Information Technology ·

8.1 Introduction

This chapter deals with the practical consequences on information technology systems arising from the introduction of European Economic and Monetary Union (EMU). Significant technological change is required to accommodate the Euro. There are also concomitant legal issues to consider, not least the issue of "Euro-compliance".

So far, the high-level political and economic debate surrounding EMU has tended to obscure other aspects in connection with the introduction of EMU. However, the practical consequences of EMU are vital.

8.2 Nature of the problem and how it will be fixed

The problem

The introduction of the Euro is not simply a matter of introducing another currency. During the transition period, transactions must be capable of being conducted interchangeably between the Euro and national denominations. Due to the special rules in relation to conversion, even existing multi-currency software packages will not (typically) be Euro-compliant. Triangulation requires two currency conversions for a single calculation and this is not the way pre-existing software programs function. Currency conversions must be undertaken at conversion rates which are expressed as six significant figures (not decimal places). Systems will also need to be introduced to address the different conventions of numerical expression of numbers between continental Europe and the United Kingdom, *e.g.* 1000,01 versus 1,000.01.

The problem surrounding EMU is complex and will vary from business to business. Unlike the Year 2000 problem, which is inherently technical, the introduction of the EMU gives rise to a functionality problem.

---

* This chapter was written by Victoria Bright, Partner and Usha Jagessar, Associate, Dibb Lupton Alsop.

In other words, computer systems which are not EMU compliant will not actually fail but will be effectively useless if they can only perform functions in respect of existing national currencies and are unable to perform functions in connection with the Euro. To resolve this functionality problem software and hardware will need to be upgraded or modified, which in turn gives rise to technical issues.

The technical issues involved will, of course, vary depending on the type of software used, the business function for which the software is used and to what extent this software interfaces with internal and external systems. For instance, the reliance of so many entities on historical financial data for analysing performance, price calculations, risk measurement, credit evaluation and trend prediction (to name but a few examples), means that when a business changes over to the Euro, all relevant historical financial data denominated in the national currency unit will have to be converted to Euros. This poses significant problems for virtually all financial information systems, including those with foreign currency functionality, as such functionality will not typically extend to multiplying or dividing historical balances by a fixed conversion rate.

"Trickledown" effect

In spite of the UK Government ruling out joining EMU during the lifetime of this Parliament, UK companies with branches or subsidiaries and customers or suppliers or competitors in participating States will find it necessary to adapt or modify their systems to cope with the Euro. There will be significant "spill over" of Euros into the UK economy as businesses that deal in Euros start paying and accounting in that currency. The Euro currency is not available initially but electronic payments in Euro can and are being made already. Many of the large multinationals operating in the United Kingdom have already indicated they will be switching all their treasury operations to the Euro.

Thus, even where software is used purely for domestic purposes within the United Kingdom it will be necessary to upgrade or amend software to be Euro-compliant.

Big bang or parallel running approach?

There are several strategies possible for the conversion of systems from current domestic currencies to the Euro during the transition period.

What is known as the "big bang" approach involves the conversion from the national currency to the Euro at a certain time and on a certain date. This will involve selecting a particular "cross-over" date and implementing appropriate software to effect the conversion. This process will mean that all existing "historical" data will be converted into Euros at one time.

In contrast to the conversion entailed in the big bang approach, the "parallel running" approach involves systems running both existing currencies and the Euro at the same time during the transition period. This approach will require increased software functionality and improved hardware to cope with the vast processing capacity needed for the multi-processing that will be necessary.

On balance, in spite of the relative cost effectiveness of the big bang approach compared to the parallel running approach, it would appear that a significant number of organisations will tend towards the latter approach.

Parallel running offers the advantage of systems being capable of processing both the existing currency as well as the Euro during the transition stage until the introduction of the new currency parallel running provides a clear comparison of the existing currency against the Euro allowing for accurate analysis and reporting. It also allows for dual book-keeping and avoids potential difficulties that may arise from conversion of all historical data without any regulatory framework in place. Most importantly this approach will allow systems the capability of reverting back to the existing currencies with ease were EMU to fail.

As an alternative to the above methods of conversion, it is possible to adopt an approach which combines elements of both the big bang and the parallel running approach, whereby a phased conversion takes place. This would require the implementation of software applications and interface applications for gradual cross-over from existing currencies to the Euro.

8.3 Areas likely to be affected

General

The software packages that are most likely to require adaptation or modification were considered by the European Commission at the end of 1997 to comprise of the following:

- accounting software (general ledger);
- electronic payment systems;
- invoicing and billing systems;
- payroll systems;
- accounts receivable and accounts payable sub-ledgers;
- inventory sub-ledgers, which record the value of the inventory;
- fixed asset sub-ledgers, which keep track of the fixed assets, their value, and calculate the depreciation charge for the period;
- work in progress;
- financial planning and budgeting software;
- costing systems;
- enterprise resource planning (ERP) systems;
- treasury management systems; and
- legal databases containing financial contracts.

8.4 Technical issues

One Euro to a six significant figure

When converting the Euro to national currencies, the Euro shall be expressed in terms of the respective national currency to six significant figures. The full conversion rate must be applied for the conversion and must not be rounded or truncated when making the conversion.

Triangulation rule

In order to convert from one currency to another it will be necessary first to convert the currency into Euros at the official exchange rate and then convert from Euros into the desired currency. Thus, converting French francs into Deutschmarks, for example, now requires a conversion from French francs into Euros and a subsequent conversion from Euros into Deutschmarks. This "triangulation rule" for conversion is set out in Article 4 of the Article 235 (new Article 308) Regulation (Council Regulation (EC) 1103/97). Software will have to be able to cope with this two-stage conversion (and subsequent rounding) rather than the typical simple conversion which exists from one currency to another.

Rounding of national currency or Euro further to conversion

When a national currency is converted to the Euro or the Euro is converted to a national currency, the amount must be rounded up to the nearest Euro cent or sub-unit of currency, as set out in Article 5 of the Article 235 (new Article 308) Regulation (Council Regulation 1103/97). This is necessary to prevent fractions of currency. Software systems will need to be able to meet these rounding requirements without any complicated authorisations which are usually required to prevent fraud.

Historical data

The Euro has no historical data for use as a means of reference or analysis upon which to assess future business performance. Organisations will have to select historical data which may be key to assessing business performance as a means of evaluating the correlation between Euro rates and other rates on a hypothetical construction of historical data. This will be a particularly demanding challenge and will rely on the successful and appropriate conversion of historical data. Software will be required to implement this synthesis of historical data. The comparison generated will also be subject to the effect of the rounding and triangulation regulations, which the software will need to accommodate.

Euro symbol, keyboards

Software must be capable of generating Euro symbols and such symbols should also be included on the standard keyboard. In some instances, third party software can be installed to upgrade software applications in respect of the Euro symbols.

Interfaces with other software products and systems

Where systems need to interface with each other, difficulties are likely to arise where one system is Euro-compliant and the other is not. Such difficulties can, however, be overcome by various methods such as building interfaces which convert the different currency units between systems; or making all interfacing systems Euro-compliant simultaneously (*i.e.* the big bang approach) to prevent the need for "converter interfaces'.

8.5 Existing systems

Contracts relating to existing systems must be reviewed to check to see whether there are any provisions in respect of Euro-compliance.

Off-the-shelf software

Companies will need to contact the relevant supplier to ask whether the Euro issue is being addressed and, if it is, the timescales involved. If the relevant supplier is not planning to address this issue, companies may have little choice but to replace the software. The existing contract with the relevant supplier should then be examined carefully to ascertain whether or not a claim to cover the cost of upgrading or installing alternative software can and should be brought against that supplier.

Bespoke software

More often than not, companies will not own bespoke software. They will be licensed to use such software and then only in "object code" (the machine readable code) as opposed to the "source code" (the human readable code).

A company in this position will almost certainly have its hands tied when it comes to amending or altering the software, either because the terms of the licence prohibit it or because it cannot do so without the source code. Unless specific provision is made in the agreement, any escrow arrangements between the company and the owner or licensor of the source code are unlikely to help in these circumstances because escrow release is usually triggered only if the supplier becomes insolvent or fails to provide maintenance. If there are no escrow arrangements between the parties and the source code can no longer be found, new systems may need to be considered.

Embedded software

As hardware contains embedded software, companies must give due consideration to the question of whether or not it is possible to adapt such embedded software to deal with the Euro.

8.6 Legal issues with existing systems

It will be difficult to claim against a supplier for non-compliance where a system has been provided under a contract containing no provisions in connection with Euro-compliance.

However, in circumstances in which software should be able to cope with the Euro but the contract does not contain an express provision that the software is Euro-compliant, then the customer may be able to rely on an implied term in the contract.

The ability to imply a Euro-compliant provision into a contract will depend on the date on which the contract was entered. For instance, if the contract was entered into more than, say, three years ago the supplier should have an argument that it was unreasonable for the software to have been Euro-compliant.

Whereas a claim for breach of contract for software developed for use in connection with European currencies, which is not in fact Euro-compliant, will be more successful if it was entered into within the last year.

The following elements will be necessary for a successful claim:

- the claim not being time-barred;
- a contract being in place and/or a duty of care existing between the supplier and the customer;
- Euro-compliance being an express or implied term of that contract and/or Euro-compliance forming part of the duty of care between the supplier and the customer;
- evidence that there was a breach of such a contract and/or there was a breach of a duty of care;
- establishing that the supplier's liability has not been limited or excluded by other express terms in the contract or notices excluding liability in tort; and
- establishing that the supplier's breach has caused the customer direct foreseeable loss.

8.7 New systems

All new systems purchased should now be Euro-compliant, however, there is still no clear definition of what Euro-compliance means. Some obvious elements include the ability of the system to implement correctly the conversion (including triangulation) and rounding requirements, and to perform all of its monetary functions in Euros. What is clear is that due diligence, supplier certification and appropriate warranties will all play an important role when purchasing new systems as indeed will a clearly defined statement of requirements by businesses.

8.8 Legal issues with new systems

IT contracts

Best practice procedures are required to the same degree as in any IT procurement contract in an attempt to achieve protection for both the supplier and the customer in connection with Euro-compliance. The following are of principal importance in relation to the contract:

Euro requirement provision

A specification of the appropriate level of Euro-compliance will have to be incorporated. This will vary according to the nature and size of the organisation involved and will have to be drafted and "scoped" accordingly.

Euro warranties

Companies purchasing or licensing new IT systems which need to have the capability to handle the Euro must ensure that appropriate warranties are contained in the related IT contracts to provide some level of assurance that the software is Euro-compliant. The usual software warranties are either express or implied.

Express warranties
These are required to provide a minimum level of assurance that the software will meet certain standards. It is desirable that any Euro warranty given by a software supplier is in an express form rather than relying on an implied term in the contract. The level of assurance given will depend on several factors, such as whether the customer has a complex system that requires a high level of Euro-compliance or whether a lower level will suffice, the relative bargaining strengths of the parties and whether all necessary functionality required to deal with EMU-related issues is comprehensively set out in the functional specification.

There are clearly difficulties in assessing the required level of Euro-compliance due to the subjectivity of the meaning of Euro-compliance. There is no single universal definition of Euro-compliance due to the individual Euro requirements varying from business to business. As such, many organisations appear to prefer warranties in relation to a specification with which the software, hardware, product or service must comply. Clearly, for this approach to be effective, there must be proper co-operation between the author of the technical specifications for the software and the person drafting the contract.

Where a thorough specification is given which addresses the specific requirements of the particular customer there is little need to rely on protection from warranties to be implied into a contract where software proves to be non-compliant. In other words, where a specification fully covers the required level of Euro-compliance needed by the customer and there is an express warranty in relation to this specification then the customer should be adequately protected.

Some customers may require software to be Euro-compliant but without reference to a detailed specification. In such cases general Euro warranties can be adopted. Some software developers such as the Business and Accounting Software Developers Association (BASDA) have devised their own general Euro-compliance warranties in terms of the following:

Euro warranties for the benefit of the customer. The warranty should state that the licensor represents, warrants and undertakes that the software will be:

- capable of performing all functions set out in the software specification for any number of currencies and for the common currency used by members of the European Union and for the Euro;
- capable of accepting, displaying and printing all Euro symbols and codes which may be adopted by any government or any other European Union body in relation to the Euro or any other currency;
- compliant with all legal requirements currently in place or hereafter applicable to the Euro in any jurisdiction including but not limited to the rules on conversion, triangulation and rounding set out in Council Regulation (EC) 1103/97 and any subsequent or similar Regulation or law;

- compliant with all laws and regulations applicable in the United Kingdom including those applicable to the introduction of the Euro or any other country in the European Union.

Euro warranties for the benefit of the supplier. The warranty should state that:

(1) The licensor warrants that the software is capable of being operated in difference currencies.

(2) The licensor intends that the software will be capable of supporting the requirements of the EMU regulations as soon as practical after these regulations are fully known.

(3) The customer is responsible for ensuring that the fully integrated system is EMU compliant.

Implied warranties

The significance of implied warranties depends on whether software is considered to qualify as "goods" and therefore, whether the software will benefit from the more extensive implied warranties and consequent protection provided under the Sale of Goods Act 1979. If software is considered to qualify as goods under this Act then the software will have to be of satisfactory quality and be fit for the purpose in reference to its specification. This is a higher standard than the warranties implied into a contract for the provision of services.

There has been much debate as to whether software qualifies as goods or services. The most significant judicial opinion was that held in the *St Albans* case (*St Albans* v *ICL* [1996] 4 All ER 481) which supported the view that software, in many situations, qualifies as goods rather than a service, in particular when software is provided on disk or as part of an entire computer system.

Change management clause

This would be included for the benefit of software suppliers. If a supplier is only capable of offering software with Euro functionality to a certain level of compliance it may be necessary to make any additional functionality the subject of such a clause. It would be especially prudent to include such a clause in countries which have not yet introduced the Euro, so as to allow for any additional Euro functionality which is required in the software, but has not been achieved by the supplier.

Liability clauses

A customer should have the benefit of a reasonable liability clause on the basis of an assessment of the loss accrued should the system fail, due to failure of the software, as a result of its non-compliance.

The clause should set a ceiling for sums refundable where a system has failed; set out additional costs required to be paid by the customer (if necessary) for a replacement product; include any further costs that may be required by the supplier for repair of the product; and provide details of loss of revenue, profits or anticipated earnings should the product fail. Such specific details are particularly important in light of the Court of Appeal decision of *British Sugar plc* v *NEI Power Projects Ltd and Another* [1998] ITCLR 118 which confirmed the importance of setting out specific parameters of liability rather than relying on an undefined exclusion for "consequential loss".

Copyright ownership

The process of modifying existing software to make it Euro-compliant will involve modification to the source code. Source code is usually protected by copyright. This means that a company will need to satisfy itself that it has the legal right to use the relevant source code for the purpose of making any changes which it requires to make the software Euro-compliant.

Such legal right means permission (typically in the form of a licence), from the owner of the copyright in the source code to make the relevant changes. Under section 11(2) of the Copyright, Designs and Patents Act 1988 the copyright in software created by an employee, in the ordinary course of that employee's employment, will automatically be owned by their employer.

However, where an organisation has entered into a software development agreement with an independent third party (*e.g.* consultant) for the development of software tailored specifically for that organisation, "bespoke software", then under section 11(1) of the Copyright, Designs and Patents Act 1988 the third party will usually own the copyright in that software, unless there is a provision in the relevant software development agreement vesting all intellectual property rights in the organisation.

There should therefore, always be an express provision vesting all intellectual property rights in organisations which commission the development of software from independent contractors. Often in a situation in which an organisation has commissioned, and thus paid a third party to develop software, then in the absence of such an express provision, an implied licence may be deemed to be in place. This means that the organisation may have access to the software source code and may therefore have the legal right to modify the source code. That said, there could be complications with such an implied licence, particularly in circumstances where the organisation does not have the ability itself to make the relevant changes and would therefore need to employ a third party for this purpose. For example, there may be confidentiality provisions preventing a disclosure of the source code to such third party.

It is therefore, important that the organisation checks the terms of any software development agreement to see whether title to the copyright has passed to them or indeed, where an employee has developed the software that this was, in fact, done within the scope of their employment. Where the "employee" is in fact a subcontractor under a contract for services, the services contract should specify that the organisation will own all intellectual property rights created during the term of the contract.

In the case of software which was not developed specifically for an organisation, "off-the-shelf software", the organisation will probably be using the software under a licensing arrangement (*e.g.* shrink-wrap licence). It is unlikely that in these circumstances the organisation will be given special permission under the terms of the licence to modify the source code.

That said, in order to assist in its internal "Euro-planning" programme the organisation should make enquiries with the shrink-wrap licensor, in order to ascertain whether and, if so, when the licensor plans to introduce Euro-functionality in its software.

Escrow agreements

An escrow arrangement involves the source code being kept secure by a trusted third party. Such an arrangement is implemented for the benefit of the licensee when the licensee does not have the right to access the source code under the software development agreement. The escrow agreement will provide the licensee access to the source code in the event that the licensor is unable to perform its obligations under the software development agreement to the licensee's detriment.

The trusted third party will be allowed to release the source code to the licensee upon certain trigger events, such as the insolvency of the licensor.

Existing escrow agreements are unlikely to include non Euro-compliance as a trigger event. The National Computing Centre (NCC) standard escrow agreement only covers failure to maintain and insolvency as trigger events. The parties can agree their own list of trigger events however, and accordingly it may be appropriate to negotiate escrow agreements that will trigger the release of the source code in the event of non Euro-compliance.

8.9 Practical steps for businesses

As with the Year 2000 problem, all companies should conduct a detailed systems audit to identify which software programs will be affected by the Euro and who is responsible for those programs. Legal considerations will clearly be a factor in determining how the problem is dealt with and, in particular, who is liable to pay for any necessary modifications. But legal considerations alone will not determine who is responsible for paying, simply because (depending upon the timescales involved) this is not a problem which should have been anticipated and dealt with by suppliers when agreements were entered into in the same way as the Year 2000 problem.

Practical solutions are needed which must be implemented and fully tested very quickly, regardless of the fact that many of the required modifications to accounting and banking systems will be highly complex. The following strategy will help in achieving EMU-compliance:

(1) The introduction of the Euro should be planned as a major event with the full sponsorship of the board and senior management.

(2) Responsibility must be delegated to one person within each organisation who will be required to collate information about EMU and the changeover to the Euro, and who will disseminate that information to the relevant organisational head.

(3) An overall steering committee should be established to co-ordinate activities across the company, approve any changes to business, marketing or operational strategy and, where necessary, to arbitrate between various organisational units.

(4) A comprehensive software inventory must be undertaken (including end-user applications like spreadsheets) linked to an impact matrix which shows the effect of various single currency issues.

(5) A risk register should be prepared showing the internal and external dependencies of the required changes and how these will be managed.

(6) Year 2000 experiences should be drawn on whenever possible.

This vital analysis work will assist companies in assessing the way in which the Euro will impact on the fundamental business strategy and/or processes of the company and the changes it will create in the market in which it operates.

8.10 Conclusion

Monetary union in Europe clearly creates new challenges for businesses and also the IT industry. It is more complex than decimalisation 25 years ago. Its effects stretch right across the organisation and beyond into the marketplace in which a company operates. As the Euro will be the currency of our biggest single export market it will affect UK companies whether or not the United Kingdom opts in or out. It is important that all UK companies now undertake a review of their current business strategies and operations to assess the impact of the EMU under both a "UK in" and a "UK out" scenario, and take the steps necessary to ensure that they are well prepared. Part of those steps may well be to modify, replace or outsource existing systems to enable them to cope with the Euro.

*Chapter 9**

· Euroland and the USA ·

9.1 Introduction

This chapter aims to set out the various legal arguments surrounding the effect of the introduction of the Euro on the continuity of contracts governed by New York law but denominated in the old currency of one of the 11 Member States of the European Union (EU) which have adopted the Euro. The current state of the law makes it very difficult to give any concrete answers regarding the current legal position of such contracts. However, after considering the relevant legal theory sections of the text of the recently enacted New York Statute on the Euro will be set out and a brief analysis of its provisions given.

One of the major legal issues related to the introduction of the Euro is the uncertainty surrounding the continuity of contracts denominated in the currencies of those EU Member States which have adopted the Euro. These national currencies (NCUs) have effectively become sub-units of the Euro for the transitional period and will cease to exist from 1 January 2002. In the absence of specific legislation to the contrary it may be argued that contracts denominated in the national currencies of the States that have adopted the Euro would be frustrated due to impossibility of performance after the introduction of the Euro.

The EU has attempted to solve this problem and prevent there being any uncertainty by the enactment of Article 3 of the Article 235 (new Article 308) Regulation which states:

> "The introduction of the Euro shall not have the effect of altering any term of a legal instrument or of discharging or excusing performance under any legal instrument, nor give a party the right unilaterally to alter or terminate a legal instrument. This provision is subject to anything which the parties may have agreed."

The Regulation defines "legal instruments" as "legislative and statutory provisions, acts of administration, judicial decisions, contracts,

---

* This chapter was written by Mike Pullen, Associate, Dibb Lupton Alsop, Brussels

unilateral legal acts, payment instruments other than banknotes and coins, and other instruments with legal effect".

This means that the legal status of existing contracts denominated in NCUs will not change after the introduction of the Euro in the absence of an express agreement between the parties to alter or discharge the contract in question.

9.2 The transitional period

Council Regulation 974/98

The rules dealing with the transitional period are set out in Article 8 of Regulation 974/98, which provides that payments during the transitional period 1 January 1999 to 31 December 2001 may be discharged in NCUs or in Euros.

Article 8(3) of the Regulation provides that debts under a contract can be discharged in certain instances in either Euros or NCUs so that any amount denominated in NCUs which is payable within the Member State of the relevant NCU, *e.g.* French Francs to be paid in a contract in France may be paid either in Euros or that NCU. Therefore, an obligation in a contract under Belgian francs payable in Brussels may be discharged either in Belgian francs or Euros. Similarly, an obligation payable in Euros may be discharged in Euros or Belgian francs. But a French franc obligation payable in Germany may only be paid in French francs. This is because it is not payable in the State of the relevant NCU, *i.e.* France.

9.3 Legal implications for contracts made under New York law

Approximately half of all worldwide contracts made on the derivatives markets are governed by New York law. Furthermore, US corporations have tended to offer Eurobonds denominated in EU currencies but the contracts are governed by New York law.

The European Commission's Green Paper on the arrangements for the introduction of the Euro (May 1995) stated that the laws of non-EU jurisdictions would recognise the Euro as a successor to the existing currencies of the 15 Member States of the EU at the fixed conversion rates set by Regulation 2866/98. The European

Commission (Commission) took the view that non-EU jurisdictions would recognise the continuity of monetary obligation and other terms of a contract, such as interest rates, on the adoption of the Euro.

9.4 **Lex monetae**

The Commission's view was to a certain extent based on the public international law doctrine of *lex monetae* or the legal theory of money. According to this doctrine, money is created by a law and it is the law of the state that issues a currency which governs what constitutes that currency and what changes may be made to the currency. A significant body of US academic opinion subscribes to the view that the US courts have applied this theory to find that an obligation under a contract to pay money is to pay what the law recognises as being money at the time the payment is made.[1] This is partly based on the decision of the New York Court of Appeals in *Dougherty* v *Equitable Life Assurance Society of the United States*.[2] In this case the court relied on an exchange rate fixed by the Soviet Government. The US courts have held that contracts for the payment of money are subordinated to the constitutional power over currency of the government.

The US courts have also recognised that there is a legitimate application of power by a sovereign government where it fixed the conversion rate at which an old currency is substituted by a new currency and provided for the discharge of debts originally denominated in the old currency at a fixed conversion rate to the new currency. In *Trinh* v *Citibank NA*[3] the court, in a contractual dispute, applied the Vietnamese currency law to convert an old Vietnamese currency into new Vietnamese currency under the official convergence rate.

However Gruson states that in both *Dougherty* and *Trinh* the contracts at issue were governed under foreign law (Russian and Vietnamese respectively). He argues that, had the contracts been governed under New York law or the law of another US state, the outcome may have been different. He concludes that no US court has had the opportunity to rule on point as to whether or not the doctrine of *lex monetae* applies to an agreement which is governed by the law of

1 See, *e.g.* M Gruson, *Euro-land and the World.*
2 266 NY 71, 193 NE 897 (1934), reh'g denied 266 NY 615, 195 NE 226 (1935).
3 623 F Supp 1526, 1537 (E D Mich 1985). Aff'd, 850 F 2d 1164 (6th Cir 1988).

a US state but denominated in a foreign currency. Gruson does not discount the possibility of US courts applying *lex monetae* to contracts governed by New York law but denominated in, for example, French francs now that the Euro has been introduced but he holds that there is some legal uncertainty surrounding the issue.

In contrast, Lenihan in a European Commission briefing paper, "the Legal Implications of European Monetary Union under US and New York Law" argues that the l*ex monetae* doctrine has been expressly recognised by the US Supreme Court.[4] He states that the Supreme Court has held that the power of States to use the law to determine what constitutes money is a major attribute of sovereignty both in Europe and in America. He goes on to argue that *lex monetae* has been applied on a number of occasions by the US legislature, for example, after the American civil war when the US Congress authorised the issue of paper dollars not backed by gold[5]; after the Spanish American War when Puerto Rico was absorbed into the USA and its currency was converted into US dollars; and in the depression of the 1930s when the US abandoned the Gold Standard.[6] He also states that the *lex monetae* doctrine has been applied by the US courts in cases involving a large number of currencies – most notably the Pound Sterling after Britain rejected the Gold Standard in 1931, the German Reichsmark which replaced the Austrian schilling after Germany's annexation of Austria in 1938 and the Deutschmark introduced in Germany in 1948 as a substitute currency for the Reichsmark.

Lenihan also argues that the doctrine that sovereignty over its currency extends to the use of the State's currency by non-nationals outside its jurisdiction, and includes contracts governed by the laws of other States, has received some support from the New York courts. In particular, he cites the examples of the collapse of the Russian rouble in the aftermath of World War II and the collapse of the Weimar mark in the 1920s. He states that further evidence for the recognition of the *lex monetae* doctrine by the US legal system can be found in its application by the US International Claims Commission to claims stemming from the collapse of a number of currencies after World War II (for example the Romanian lie and the Yugoslav dinar).

---

4 *Supra*, n 1.
5 *Bank* v *Supervisors*, 74 US 26 (1868).
6 *US* v *Bankers Trust Co*, 294 US 240 (1935).

In Lenihan's view the Supreme Court has taken a liberal interpretation of *lex monetae* and has held that the sovereignty of a State over its currency governs not only the regulation of monetary obligations in private contracts but is extended to govern the regulation of ancillary contractual obligations, such as interest rates which are inherently linked to monetary obligations.

It can also be argued that the US Constitution upholds the theory of *lex monetae* because it implicitly recognises that the power to establish foreign currencies is vested in foreign governments. Therefore, *lex monetae* can be treated as part of US federal law because it affects the foreign relations of the United States.

Support for the *lex monetae* doctrine can also be found in the Uniform Commercial Code (UCC) which defines money as a medium of exchange authorised or adopted by domestic or foreign governments as part of its currency. This definition of money has been adopted by all 50 states of the United States. The UCC rejects the definition that money is limited solely to legal tender and thus provides the legal basis for recognising the Euro as a sole currency issued under the law of EU Member States during the transitional period.

9.5 The act of state doctrine

Under the act of state doctrine, US courts will not rule on the validity of the acts undertaken by a foreign government within its own territories. It is clear that the act of the EU Member States in introducing the Euro as a new currency falls under the act of state doctrine and therefore should not be challenged in the US courts. Thus, it can be argued that *lex monetae* should be applied to all contracts where Article 8 of the Euro Regulation provides that obligations may be re-denominated in Euros or NCUs when the place of payment under that contract is within one of the 11 Member States in the Euro zone. However, Gruson[7] argues that the act of state doctrine will only be applied by the US courts when the contract has its *situs* in a foreign State. For example, he states that US courts have tended to find the *situs* of loan contracts in the country that is stipulated as the place of payment and the jurisdiction for the settlement of disputes is that provided for under the contract.[8] Therefore, if a contract is made in New York, governed by

---

7 *Supra*, n 1, at 16.

8 *Supra*, n 1, at 17, citing Restatement (Third) of the Foreign Relations Law of the United States (1987), s 443.

New York law and the place of payment is New York but it is denominated in Deutschmarks it is arguable that the act of state doctrine will not apply. Again the situation regarding the application of the act of state doctrine to contracts governed by New York law but denominated in NCU seems to be unclear.

9.6 Contracts not void or voidable or unenforceable

A contract denominated, for example, in Deutschmarks cannot be held to be terminated under the UCC doctrine of commercial impracticability or under common law rules on frustration, impracticability or impossibility after the introduction of the Euro. It can be argued that attempts at applying these rules would be blocked by the application of *lex monetae* by the Supreme Court. Therefore, after the introduction of the Euro in contracts governed by New York law, any contractual obligations denominated in or with reference made to national currencies of EU Member States must be discharged in Euros in line with the provisions of Article 8 of the Regulation and at the fixed conversion rate set out in Regulation 2866/98.

The rules on commercial impracticability, frustration and impossibility can only be used to justify non-performance under a contract where the performance has been frustrated, made impossible or rendered impracticable by the occurrence of an unforeseen event which could not have been anticipated at the time the contract was made. It is clear that courts are unlikely to accept any arguments that the Euro could not have been foreseen as it was enshrined in the Maastricht Treaty in 1992 and was the subject of much discussion within the European Union before that date. Furthermore, it would be difficult to argue impracticality, frustration or impossibility before a New York court when it is clear that the contract can be performed according to its terms and the parties can obtain exactly what they contracted for, *i.e.* the lawful currency of the State designated under the contract.

9.7 Force majeure clauses

The *force majeure* clauses in many contracts governed by New York law call for the payment of debts in US dollars when the currency of the contract is no longer available due to the imposition of exchange controls or other circumstances beyond the parties' control. However, such *force majeure* clauses could not be triggered by the Euro because they are designed to govern situations where a currency is in circulation but access to it is restricted by exchange control. Moreover, *force majeure* clauses can normally only be triggered by unforeseeable events.

Similarly impossibility clauses require payment in US dollars where the currency of contract is no longer used by the governments of the country issuing the currency. However, again such clauses would need to be construed in line with the state theory of money and therefore performance in Euros pursuant to Article 8 of the Regulation would generally mean that parties would not be able to rely on impossibility clauses.

There is a strong argument that the Euro falls within the general definition of money under New York law. However, problems may arise where the Euro obligations which are governed by New York law relate not only to pure monetary obligations but also to contractual obligations.

This has been recognised by the New York legislature which passed a statute providing for the continuity of contracts governed by New York law but where payments are denominated in Euros. This legislation was enacted in July 1997 and in essence confirms the continuity of contracts denominated in currencies of EU States which have joined the Euro. This is generally in line with the Council Regulation on the introduction of the Euro and US constitutional theory. Under the separation of powers doctrine a state's failure to recognise the sovereignty of the Member States of the EU over the currencies, *i.e.* the Euro, would be unconstitutional as it would infringe the federal government's authority over international monetary regulations. This means that in the event of any inconsistency between the New York legislation and the Regulation on the introduction of the Euro, US courts would construe the New York legislation in line with the Regulation because the doctrine of *lex monetae* is part of federal law.

9.8 Retroactive application of the New York legislation

On its face the New York legislation does not appear to have any retroactive effect, in that it does not seem to apply to contracts entered into before mid-1997. However, applying a liberal approach to the construction of the legislation by looking at both its history and the intent of the legislature it is clear that it was intended to apply retroactively. Again, all obligations entered into prior to 1997 must be discharged in Euros in accordance with the Regulation on the introduction of the Euro due to the application of the *lex monetae* doctrine of US federal law.

The New York legislation cannot be deemed to be unconstitutional on the grounds that it interferes with existing contracts. If the legislation is held to apply retroactively it will not impair contractual obligations because it upholds the continuity of contractual obligations in a manner that is consistent with the *lex monetae* doctrine. Furthermore, it confirms the continuity of contracts in line with the EU Regulation. Therefore, it can be argued that the legislation is declaratory of existing law and does not impair pre-existing contractual obligations. Furthermore, the legislation can be held to have been passed in order to protect a broad social interest and therefore will be upheld by the US courts.

9.9 State of New York's powers to enact legislation affecting international monetary relations

The enactment by the State of New York of legislation confirming the continuity of contracts under the Euro cannot be held to impinge upon the US federal government's undisputed authority over international monetary relations. This is due to the fact that the legislation recognises the continuity of contract in line with the Regulation on the introduction of the Euro which makes it consistent with the doctrine of lex monetae as applied by the Member States of the European Union to their currencies. Thus, the enactment of this legislation does not impinge upon the federal government's authority over international relations because it is fully consistent with the lex monetae doctrine. It is also fully consistent with the position of the federal government in respect of the EMU.

Specific provisions of the legislation

The New York Act amends Article 5 of the New York General Obligations Law. Section 5-6101 of the Act sets out the definition of the "Euro" and "the introduction of the Euro". Section 5-6102 of the Act provides as follows:

> "1(a) If a subject or medium of payment of a contract, security or instrument is a currency that has been substituted or replaced by the Euro will be a commercially reasonable substitute and substantial equivalent that may be either: (I) used in determining the value of such currency; or (II) tendered, in each case at the conversion rate specified in and otherwise calculated in accordance with, the regulations adopted by the EU.
>
> (b) If a subject or medium of payment of a contract, security or instrument is the ECU, the Euro will be a commercially reasonable substitute and substantial equivalent that may be either: (I) used in determining the value of the ECU; or (II) tendered, in each case at the conversion rate specified in, and otherwise calculated in accordance with, the regulations adopted by the Council of the European Union.
>
> (c) Performance of any of the obligations described in paragraph (a) or (b) of this subdivision may be made in the currency or currencies originally designated in such contract, security or instrument (so long as such currency or currencies remain legal tender) or in Euro, but not in any other currency, whether or not such other currency: (I) has been substituted or replaced by the Euro; or (II) is a currency that is considered a denomination of the Euro and has a fixed conversion rate with respect to the Euro.
>
> 2. None of: (a) the introduction of the Euro; (b) the tendering of Euros in connection with any obligation in compliance with paragraph (a) or (b) of subdivision one of this Section; (c) the determining of the value of any obligation in compliance with paragraph (a) or (b) of subdivision one of this Section; or (d) the calculating or determining of the subject or medium of payment of a contract, security or instrument with reference to interest rates or other basis has been substituted or replaced due to the introduction of the Euro and that is a commercially reasonable substitute and substantial equivalent, shall either have the effect of discharging or excusing performance under any contract, security or instrument, or give a party the right to unilaterally alter or terminate any contract, security or instrument."

Analysis

Section 5-1602(1)(a) clause (I) specifies that the conversion rate set by the European Council is the sole basis for valuing a NCU against the US dollar in cases where a contract calls for the valuation of an old national currency *e.g.* the French franc against the dollar.

Section 5-1602(1)(a) clause (II) deals with the transitional period in which NCUs shall continue to exist as sub-units of the Euro. It allows debtors under a contract denominated in an NCU to tender payment in Euros.

Section 5-1602(1)(b) deals with the rules on the conversion of the ECU into the Euro along the lines specified in the Council Regulation on the introduction of the Euro. This Section incorporates the presumption that references to the ECU in the Council Regulation on the introduction of the Euro which are defined are references to the official ECU. It states that the ECU and the Euro are subject to a one to one conversion rate. However, this rate may be overridden if the parties to a contract can show a contrary intention.

Section 5-1602(1)(c) follows the no compulsion/no prohibition rule set out in the Council Regulation on the introduction of the Euro. It also conforms to the transitional period for the phasing out of NCUs by limiting the right to pay in NCUs to such time as they remain legal tender. It also follows the Regulation by preventing debts denominated in one NCU from being paid in another NCU.

Section 5-1602(2) provides for the continuity of contracts and prevents the introduction of the Euro from causing contracts to be frustrated or subject to the doctrine of impossibility.

Gruson argues that the New York Act is unnecessary and that it may create confusion because it does not exactly mirror the provisions of the Regulation on the introduction of the Euro.[9] He also states that in a rapidly changing global economy the Act creates a dangerous precedent by requiring changes of currency by a foreign state to be confirmed by a New York statute rather than being automatically accepted under the doctrines of act of state and *lex monetae*.[10] It seems that Gruson is arguing that, while there may be some uncertainty surrounding the position at common law, reliance on the act of state doctrine and *lex monetae* may be a better option than the enactment of specific legislation which does not mirror the Regulation on the introduction of the Euro. Nevertheless, Gruson concludes that New York courts are almost certain to construe agreements to pay money denominated in NCUs as an agreement to pay in Euros.

9 *Supra*, n 1, at 49.
10 *Supra*, n 1 at 47-48.

9.10 Conclusion

The effect of the Euro on the continuity of contracts governed by New York law but denominated in NCUs will continue to be a grey area until the issue is litigated and a body of case law is put in place. However, at least in theory, the enactment of legislation by the State of New York means that the introduction of the Euro will not create any major difficulties for continuity of contracts governed by New York law. This is due to the fact that under the *lex monetae* doctrine all contractual obligations must be discharged in accordance with the provision of the Regulation on the introduction of the Euro. The New York State statute is broadly consistent with the Regulation and any inconsistencies between the two should be overcome by the US courts interpreting the statute in line with the Regulation. In the event of any conflict between the Regulation and the New York statute the Regulation is likely to prevail by virtue of the *lex monetae* doctrine. Therefore, contractual obligations denominated in Euros and governed by the laws of New York can be discharged pursuant to the EU Council Regulation or in accordance with the New York Act.

The New York Act may not be perfect. However, it has had the effect of dispelling much of the legal uncertainty surrounding the continuity of contracts governed by New York law but denominated in NCUs after the introduction of the Euro.[11]

---

11 It should be noted that both Pennsylvania and California have enacted similar laws to the New York statute.

· Index ·